Bloom's
GUIDES

Maya Angelou's
I Know Why the Caged Bird Sings

1984
All the Pretty Horses
Beloved
Brave New World
Cry, The Beloved Country
Death of a Salesman
Hamlet
The Handmaid's Tale
The House on Mango Street
I Know Why the Caged Bird Sings
The Scarlet Letter
To Kill a Mockingbird

Bloom's
GUIDES

Maya Angelou's
I Know Why the Caged Bird Sings

Edited & with an Introduction
by Harold Bloom

CHELSEA HOUSE
PUBLISHERS
A Haights Cross Communications Company

Philadelphia

© 2004 by Chelsea House Publishers, a subsidiary of Haights Cross Communications.

A Haights Cross Communications Company

Printed and bound in the United States of America.

First Printing
1 3 5 7 9 8 6 4 2

Library oof Congress Cataloging-in-Publication Data

Maya Angelou's I know Why the Caged Bird Sings/edited and with an introduction by Harold Bloom.
        p. cm.--(Bloom's Guides)
Includes bibliographical references and index.
  ISBN: 0-7910-7562-1 HC   0-7910-7768-3 PB
  1. Angelou, Maya. I know why the caged bird sings. 2. Authors, American--Biography--History and criticism. 3. African American authors--Biography--History and criticism. 4. Entertainers--United States--Biography--History and criticism. 5. African American entertainers--Biography--History and criticism. 6. Autobiography. I. Bloom, Harold. II. Title. III. Series
  PS3551.N464Z77 2003
  818'.5409--dc22
                                    2003012268

Chelsea House Publishers
1974 Sproul Road, Suite 400
Broomall, PA 19008-0914

www.chelseahouse.com

Contributing editor: Pamela Loos
Cover series and design by Takeshi Takahashi
Layout by EJB Publishing Services

Contents

Introduction

The popularity of *I Know Why the Caged Bird Sings* is proudly based upon its achieved pathos: It accomplishes a controlled poignance in representing a portrait of the artist as a young black woman. In the structural background of Maya Angelou's book hover the two prime traditional forms of African-American autobiography, the slave narrative and the African-American version of the church sermon. Each is at once individual and communal, with the two voices sometimes working with one another and sometimes impeding the other's full expression. Angelou, whatever her formal limitations as a poet, is a natural autobiographer who works with considerable skill and with narrative cunning. Her voice interweaves other strands in the African-American oral tradition, but the implicit forms of sermon and slave narrative are ghostly presences in her rhetoric. Angelou brings forward, with a rugged implicitness, a spiritual element vital to all indigenous American religion but original to the African-American paradigm of that religion. The early black Baptists in America spoke of "the little me within the big me," almost the last vestige of the spirituality they had carried with them on the Middle Passage from Africa. Converted to American Baptist Christianity, they brought to the slaveowner's faith a kind of gnosis, a radical knowing that "the little me" belonged not to the space and time of this harsh world but to an unfallen realm before the Creation-Fall of the whites. The sermonlike directness of *I Know Why the Caged Bird Sings* is empowered by Angelou's possession of this gnosis, which tells her always that what is best and oldest in her spirit goes back to a lost fullness of being.

Angelou's autobiographical tone is one of profound intimacy and radiates goodwill, even a serenity astonishingly at variance with the terrors and degradations she suffered as a child and as a very young woman. Her voice speaks to something in the American "little me within the big me," white and black and whatever, that can survive dreadful experiences because the deepest self is beyond experience and cannot be violated, even by such onslaughts as child abuse, rape, and prostitution. Early in this new millennium, where technocracy still renders social compassion obsolete, the prospects for the continued relevance of *I Know Why the Caged Bird Sings* are only enhanced. Despite its secular mode, the book is a spiritual autobiography that addresses the popular imagination of a nation that does not understand its own religion, a Christian gnosis that has little in common with historical European Christianity. We have no history, only biography, and our biography has the single theme: survival of the innermost self. Maya Angelou, incarnating that theme, celebrates the immortality of a deepest self that was not born, and so cannot die, and is always being resurrected.

Biographical Sketch

Maya Angelou is a writer, poet, actress, playwright, civil rights activist, film producer, and director. She lectures throughout the United States and abroad and has published several best-selling books and countless magazine articles.

She was born Marguerite Johnson on April 4, 1928, in St. Louis, to Bailey and Vivian Baxter Johnson. Her brother Bailey gave her the name Maya. When she was just three and a half, her parents divorced and sent her and her brother to Stamps, Arkansas, to live with their paternal grandmother, Annie Henderson.

Angelou describes vividly the desolate journey from California to Arkansas in the autobiography that has since brought her fame, *I Know Why the Caged Bird Sings*, published when she was 41. The book covers her life from childhood and describes the way she was raised in segregated rural Arkansas, until the birth of her son when she was 17. Her four subsequent prose books continue her life story, proceeding chronologically. In *Gather Together in My Name* (1974) she depicts her life as a teenage mother, her introduction to drugs and illicit activities, and the hardship of bare economic survival. Her young adult years as a show-business personality provide the content for *Singin' and Swingin' and Gettin' Merry Like Christmas* (1976); her life as a racial and social activist is covered in *The Heart of a Woman* (1981); her African journey from 1962 until 1965 is the topic of *All God's Children Need Traveling Shoes* (1986), and the latest installment of her autobiography, *A Song Flung Up to Heaven* (2002) explores her life after Ghana in the years between 1964 and 1968.

After graduating from Lafayette Country training school in Arkansas, Maya Angelou, along with her brother, moved to San Francisco, where she attended high school. She received a two-year scholarship to study dance and drama at the California Labor School, but in 1944 she became pregnant and gave birth to a son. In her late teens she supported herself as a Creole-style cook, nightclub waitress, and streetcar conductor.

In the early 1950s, she married Tosh Angelos. (Her last name is a variation of her then-husband's last name.) Angelos was a Greek sailor whom she met when she worked in a record store in San Francisco.

Sometime during those years, she found her way into a job as a dancer and singer. She had a winning way with audiences, and she performed in the popular West Indian Calypso style at the Purple Onion, a cabaret in San Francisco. She also appeared in the role of Ruby in *Porgy and Bess*, a U.S. Department of State-sponsored musical that toured 22 nations. She studied with Martha Graham, and, as she describes in her collection of personal essays, *Wouldn't Take Nothing for My Journey Now* (1993), she had a dancing partnership with Alvin Ailey (1933–1989) for the Al and Rita Show.

In the late '50s, after divorcing Tosh, she moved to New York City and became involved in the political and literary scene there. But her career as an actress continued to grow; it reached its high point in 1960 when she acted the White Queen in Jean Genet's satirical play, *The Blacks*. This was also the most politically active period of her life: she organized a fund-raiser called "Cabaret for Freedom" in support of Martin Luther King Jr. As a result of this, she was appointed Northern Coordinator of the Southern Christian Leadership Conference (SCLC), a position she held briefly from 1959 to 1960.

In 1961, she fell in love with a South African dissident lawyer, Vusumzi Make, and moved to Cairo with him. There, she worked as associate editor of *The Arab Observer*, the only English-language news weekly in the Middle East. After her marriage to Make ended, she moved to Ghana where she worked as assistant administrator of the School of Music and Drama with the University of Ghana.

As she depicts in *All God's Children Need Traveling Shoes*, during her time in Africa she met several people who affected her life and character. One of them was Julian Mayfield, the renowned scholar of W.E.B. Du Bois, and another was black Muslim leader El-Hajj Malik El-Shabazz, known as Malcolm X.

Two horrifying events deeply influenced Maya Angelou on her return to the United States. The first was the assassination of Malcom X on February 21, 1965, and the other was the killing of Martin Luther King in 1968.

In 1971, she published a volume of poetry, *Just Give Me a Cool Drink of Water 'fore I Diiie*, which was nominated for a Pulitzer Prize.

Her third marriage to Paul Du Feu, took place in 1973 (and ended in divorce in 1980). In 1975, President Ford appointed her to the American Revolution Council. Another book of poetry, *And Still I Rise*, was published in 1978. The next collection of poems, *I Shall Not Be Moved*, did not appear till 1990.

In the last three decades she has written and produced several prize-winning documentaries, including *Afro-Americans in the Arts*, a PBS special for which she received the Golden Eagle, and *Black, Blues, Black*, a 10-part program about the prominent role of African culture in American life. With *Georgia, Georgia*, she became the first black woman to have a screenplay produced. She also wrote the script and musical score for the television version of *I Know Why the Caged Bird Sings*. Along with all of this she has made hundreds of stage and television appearances.

In 1993, at the request of President Clinton, she delivered the poem "On the Pulse of Morning" at his inauguration. This was the first time a poet had taken part in an inauguration since Robert Frost spoke at President Kennedy's. That same year, she published *Wouldn't Take Nothing for My Journey Now*, a collection of essays on lessons in living, which, like most of its predecessors, was a best-seller. Prestigious institutions like Smith College and Mills College have granted her honorary doctorates; reportedly, she now holds fifty.

She currently resides in Winston-Salem, North Carolina, where she has a lifetime appointment as the first Reynolds Professor and Chair of American Studies at Wake Forest University.

The Story Behind the Story

Maya Angelou listened to an editor explain that it would be a good idea for her to write her autobiography and to write it as a work of literature. Angelou told him she was too busy. But when he said he believed it might be impossible to do anyway, Angelou jumped right in and said she would do it, showing herself once again as thriving on challenge. She secluded herself and worked assiduously, producing *I Know Why the Caged Bird Sings*, a work of such sensitivity and skill that it earned her a nomination for a National Book Award.

Angelou has told interviewers that it has become her habit when working on a writing project to rent a hotel room and work there, arriving by 6:30 a.m. almost daily. She writes on long yellow tablets until noon or later and then goes home to shower, have a relaxing lunch, and wind down. In the evening, she edits the work. Angelou also has spoken of the challenge and fear of drawing herself back into the past when writing her autobiographies. (*I Know Why the Caged Bird Sings* is her first autobiography in a series of six.) Luckily her memory of certain events is very powerful, and for these she can clearly recall the sights, sounds, and smells of the moment. She believes that her senses developed acutely during the period in her childhood when she was silent.

Indeed, what appeals to many readers and observers of Angelou's work is her ability to sensitively relay childhood events from a child's perspective and to write with pleasure about the sense-filled experience of life. While *I Know Why the Caged Bird Sings* has been compared to other works in the black American autobiographical tradition, it is agreed that this book goes beyond the techniques typically seen in this genre and that it is universal. Black American male autobiographers have written of the search for freedom and education; of the importance of community and the adoption of black pride as a coping mechanism against oppression; of family, nurturing, and the quest for self-sufficiency, personal dignity, and self definition. Angelou and other black women address these concerns and also address specifically female issues. For example, throughout Angelou's book her younger self is concerned with how she looks, and for most of the text she sees herself as ugly for being non-white and non-feminine. Yet as the young girl struggles with growing up and becomes more knowledgeable, she does develop a positive self-image; she comes to the realization that she can control her own life and to do so must rely on her own strong intellect. In this way she also breaks from the slave narratives that describe a journey through chaos, for Angelou realizes she must take the chaos and create her own order.

Like other black female authors, Angelou also writes of the black female's need to cope with men, black and white alike. The greatest tragedy described in her book, for example, is a confrontation not of white against black but of black male adult against black female child, bringing out into the open problems within the black community itself. Some critics have commented on the fact that Angelou's job as a writer is tougher than most since she attempts to write for both black and white audiences. Certainly her continued popularity with a diverse audience is a testament to her ably meeting this challenge.

Critics also comment on Angelou's weaving various forms into her work. We know from her autobiography that she was a lover of literature from a very young age, appreciating it, looking to it for answers, and finding it a great escape and anchor. Her use of various forms within her own work further exemplifies her delight in the written word. For example, within this autobiography she relates sermons, a ghost story, a children's rhyme, and both secular and religious songs. Her concern with form is also apparent when one examines her methods of structuring consecutive chapters, a chapter itself, or different related sections within the book.

Prominent in her work is also her struggle to find her own way for handling white oppression of blacks. While one critic has remarked that Maya for the most part is an observer of Southern prejudice rather than a direct victim of it, Angelou's sensitivity in describing the black's life remains startlingly vivid. Her deftness radiates in her ability to portray great horrors yet still transcend them. In addition to this, she shows her talent in her lyrical imagery, self-parody, humor, compassion, portraiture, and storytelling technique, enveloping her reader in a story of poignant realism and hope.

List of Characters

Marguerite Johnson is also called Margaret, Ritie, My, and Maya. The narrator of the book, for the most part she speaks from her childhood perspective. She describes her childhood fears, pains, and needs, all of which are compounded by the additional burden of being black and sent away by divorced parents. She shines because of her love of life, sensitivity, and ability to transcend intense hardship.

Bailey, Maya's brother, is one year older than she. The two have their own world of jokes and secrets and also have an intense bond. Bailey has more courage and charm than Maya, and she sees him as always knowing what to do. He is a strong source of support, innately understanding her hostile feelings about their parents and offering her his advice on how to handle her first white boss and when to tell their mother about her pregnancy.

Annie Henderson, whom the children call "Momma," is Maya's grandmother (her father's mother), who raises the children for many years. Maya sees her as the embodiment of great strength. She is stern and determined to rear the children properly and also has the sensitivity and wherewithal to help Maya out of her muteness. She is not formally educated but is full of wisdom, highly religious, hard-working, a great entrepreneur, and quite extraordinary as one of the few black women in Stamps at the time who owned land and a store.

Vivian Baxter, is Maya's mother, beauty personified in Maya's eyes. She is fiercely tough and independent and makes money by running card games. She is the modern city woman living the blues lifestyle. Concerned about providing for her children, she is not so concerned about watching over them.

Bailey Johnson, Sr., is Maya's father, who is tall and handsome, feigns importance, and wants to appear smooth yet usually

15

speaks in a halting manner. He is insensitive to his children, sending them off to their mother with almost no warning, later laughing when Maya does not get along with his girlfriend, and forcing his daughter to fend for herself in a foreign country while he disappears to get drunk.

Uncle Willie is Maya's uncle and one of Momma's two sons. He lives with Momma, is crippled, and stutters. He believes in Momma's philosophies and harsh child-rearing tactics, threatening to push the children against a hot stove when they miss in reciting their multiplication tables and whipping them with switches after they lose control in church. While blacks are trapped by society's oppression, Uncle Willie is also trapped in a disfigured body, and so Maya feels a kinship with him.

Angelou calls **Mrs. Bertha Flowers** her lifeline. Mrs. Flowers is the wealthy, sophisticated, and sensitive woman who pulls Maya out of her muteness through books and attention to the young girl. The woman teaches Maya practical lessons about life and also broadens her appreciation of literature, which serves as a great help for Maya throughout the book. Mrs. Flowers is one of the few adults whom Maya admires and thoroughly respects.

The Baxter family is composed of powerful figures, most notably Maya's Grandmother Baxter, who has connections with the police and uses these to trade favors with the St. Louis underground. Her sons are repeatedly described as mean, and we assume they are responsible for Mr. Freeman's death, although this is never explicitly stated.

Mr. Freeman lives with Vivian Baxter when Maya and Bailey are relocated to St. Louis. He is much older than Vivian, and Maya says he is lucky to have her as his girlfriend. Usually quiet, he comes to life with Mother. He rapes Maya and threatens to kill her brother if she tells anyone about it. Mr.

Freeman represents the destroyed black male and asserts his limited power to prey upon children.

Daddy Clidell marries Vivian, and the children live with the new couple the second time they move away from Stamps. Like the Baxters, Daddy Clidell is most comfortable in the underground. He and his con-men friends teach the children how they outwit whites, so the children themselves can never be victimized by such tricks.

Summary and Analysis

> "What you looking at me for?
> I didn't come to stay … "

These lines of poetry begin the **prologue** of *I Know Why the Caged Bird Sings*. They are voiced and repeated in church by the young Maya Angelou, who is intensely embarrassed as she is unable to recall what she must recite next, provoking giggles from her peers. The lines serve as a foreshadowing of themes and experiences to come: the need to break free of humiliation over one's physical attributes; the struggle of growing up and developing an identity; the combat with racism; the driving desire for a home and its love, security, and unconditional acceptance; and coping mechanisms.

Stuck in a limbo of forgetfulness, Maya hears her rustling taffeta dress and recalls her earlier dream that the dress is magic. As she had watched her grandmother fix it, she "knew" she would look like a movie star in it, "like one of the sweet little white girls who were everybody's dream of what was right with the world." But in the light of Easter morning, she realizes her miracle is illusory. She no longer sees the dress as magical but as an ugly, faded discard from a white woman. Yet she persists in imagining that one day she will snap out of her "black ugly dream" and surprise the world with her long blond hair and light-blue eyes.

Yanked back to her embarrassing reality by the minister's wife, who feeds Maya her final line of poetry, the young girl blurts out the last line and then realizes she has to go to the toilet, quite urgently. She attempts to regain some composure and tiptoes toward the back of the church, only to trip over a child's foot and to feel urine running down her legs. Rushing out into the yard and toward her house crying, she knows she will be punished and teased but laughs anyway, at the "sweet release" and her escape from the "silly church."

The events of the prologue, not occurring in their proper chronological spot in the autobiography, gain much attention, and rightfully so. The young Maya's laughing at an institution traditionally seen as a haven for blacks foreshadows her need to find her own way and not rely on a sanctuary that she views as not providing enough help. Her embarrassment over her body will remain a key issue throughout the book as well, and her inability to speak will later appear as a self-imposed muteness. The child escapes the church in laughter, just as the author will use humor at other points in the text as a relief from intense events described in the book.

Chapter one opens with a description of the three-year-old Maya and her four-year-old brother Bailey arriving in the small southern town of Stamps, Arkansas, having been shuttled off by their divorcing parents to live with their grandmother. Bailey's name is stated without an explanation of who he is, as if he is so much a part of Maya's life he almost is an extension of herself and therefore needs no introduction (which we will soon find to be the case). The children are haunted by their parents' rejection through most of the book. Not only have they been sent away from their parents and home to a place they hardly know, but they travel by themselves on the long trek from California. Literally, they are labeled like baggage or mail, with tags on their wrists addressed "To Whom It May Concern" and stating their names, addresses, and destination.

The first description upon their arrival is not of their greeting by their grandmother and their uncle, with whom she lives, but of the town's reaction to the children. The imagery reminds us of the children's hunger for love. The town is described as reacting to them "as a real mother embraces a stranger's child. Warmly, but not too familiarly." In short, they still feel unloved. Their literal rejection from their parents' home provokes a longing for a new home, a place that will offer acceptance and love; the loss of home also batters their self worth, for, after all, if their own parents do not love them, what value do they have? In an effort to create some normal childhood experience, the two wayfarers soon start calling their grandmother "Momma."

In this chapter, their grandmother is shown as a successful, smart entrepreneur, owning a general store that is the center of activities in the black part of town. For Maya, it is initially a fun place that becomes one of her favorites. Her grandmother is also shown as religious and industrious. She rises at four o'clock daily, immediately thanks God for not having taken her life overnight, and asks him to "help me to put a bridle on my tongue." Her thanks for not bringing death indicates humble expectations. The request for a bridled tongue mirrors the muteness Maya later experiences and Maya's idea that words can be uncontrollably evil and even cause death.

The store is a gathering place in the morning, when the black workers are full of hope about how much cotton they will pick. Yet at the end of the day, in the "dying" sun, their "supernatural" expectations are ruined by reality—not enough cotton picked, weighted scales, and sacks that will have to be sewn overnight with already sore, stiff fingers. Young Maya is shown here as keenly observant as well as empathic. Later, the author tells us, she would experience "inordinate rage" whenever she saw stereotyped presentations of happy-go-lucky cotton pickers. Such anger is something she will learn to give voice to as she grows in the book. Also notable here is the author's framework of the day that starts hopeful and fades to pain. She uses nature imagery and will show her strength with this technique at other points in the text as well.

A focus on the significant intelligence of the two children (still only five and six years old) both starts and ends **chapter two**. In the beginning the focus is on math, and at the end it is about literature. Indeed, literature will be a great aid for Maya throughout the book and will be a major savior after her traumatic rape at a young age. The chapter opens with Maya and Bailey expertly reciting the multiplication tables. Uncle Willie officiates, pushing them near the burning red pot-bellied stove if they make too many errors.

Just as the description of their grandmother consumed most of chapter one, Uncle Willie is described in most of this chapter. This is when we learn that he is crippled—crooked in posture, with a distorted face and one small hand, and unable to walk without a cane. He is made fun of by both children and black men, who struggled to make the barest minimum and were jealous of Uncle Willie, working in a bountiful store with a starched shirt and shining shoes. A rather lengthy description is given of one time when the young Maya watched Uncle Willie pretend that he was not lame. She never learns why at that moment he decided to do so, but again she shows great sympathy for him and others like him, comparing him to a prisoner who is tired of bars and the guilty who tire of blame. Her empathy is so intense that she tells us this is the closest she has ever felt to Uncle Willie, and we recognize that she herself feels helpless and trapped with no possible method of escape. This is just one example of her compassion for others as well as her keen ability to create portraits of people.

Just as in chapter one, where the town's inhabitants are compared to a parent, so, too, here Uncle Willie is compared to a father. Despite the scary punishment he threatens by the stove, Maya sees him as better than her real father. "In fact," she writes, "I would have pretended to be his daughter if he wanted me to. Not only did I not feel any loyalty to my own father, I figure that if I had been Uncle Willie's child I would have received much better treatment." Again we see the primal urge for a parent, even a flawed one. At the same time, we see Maya rejecting her true father, preparing us for her later reactions to him. She has no magical hope for her father or their relationship, no empathy for him like she has for others.

The chapter ends with Maya explaining how she "met and fell in love with William Shakespeare." The word choice almost makes the reader feel Shakespeare is alive. Maya wants us to recognize how alive his writing makes her feel. Yet even at this young age she believes she has to keep this love a secret, since he is a white man and her grandmother would not accept this.

Just as she felt strong empathy with Uncle Willie's plight, and we are not given a clear explanation as to why, here she explains a great attraction to particular lines of Shakespeare and we must discern why. "When in disgrace with fortune and men's eyes" are his words that she says describe a state with which she is most familiar. This fits in with the feeling portrayed in the prologue and that will persist at other points in the book.

The store is Maya's favorite place all the way through age thirteen. In **chapter three** she explains her pleasure in opening the front doors like "pulling the ribbon off the unexpected gift," in becoming expert in measuring out just the right amount of dry goods, in experiencing the rhythms of the day among the mackerel, salmon, tobacco, and thread. Many critics comment on Angelou's descriptive skill, and she sensually describes here her love for pineapples and the blissful peace of having dinner at the back of the store. After a day's work, even Uncle Willie's disabilities seem to disappear, and feeding smelly slop to the hogs after dinner doesn't seem to be such a chore.

The pleasures described in this chapter's beginning stand in sharp contrast to the rest of the chapter, which is thick with fear and humiliation. The children overhear Momma being warned by a former sheriff that Uncle Willie should hide because the Ku Klux Klan will be out that night searching for the black man that "messed with" a white woman that day. Angelou provides her reaction years after the event amid the description of the event, which is told from the child's perspective in the real time of her book. Some critics find this technique disturbing, while others believe Angelou manages it quite well. She is sickened by the facts that the former sheriff is proud of himself for providing the warning and that he feels no responsibility for stopping the rampage. Each black man is in danger of losing his life, even one who is seriously crippled. The family immediately sets about emptying the bin that holds potatoes and onions, so that Uncle Willie can squeeze his already misshapen body into it. They cover him with layer upon layer of vegetables and hear him moaning throughout the night. Maya is sure he would have been lynched, if the "boys" they were warned about had forced Momma to open the store. Very early in the book, then, we see the horrible fear that the evilness of whites causes.

A rather lengthy description of Mr. McElroy, who lives next to the store, opens **chapter four**. He is notable to the young Maya for being one of the few black men she knows who wears suits. He is an independent black man who owns his land and a large house—"a near anachronism in Stamps." He is a man who keeps to himself but enjoys Uncle Willie's company. Also in his favor, Angelou tells us, is the fact that he never went to church. She and Bailey already must feel the pressure of following the Christian religion in this small town and question its necessity, for they view Mr. McElroy as "courageous" for not giving in to it. Little Maya actually views this as such a formidable act that she excitedly watches him for signs of his next incredible move; he remains a mystery to the child.

Directly following this description of a puzzling, heroic neighbor is the first portrait of Bailey, "the greatest person in my world," according to Maya. Upon reading this glowing testimonial, one is forced to question why it took so long to appear. Why, for example, is a relatively minor next-door neighbor examined first? Perhaps the baffling adult world needs attention first, and a brave adult is the perfect segue to her brother.

At the onset, Maya compares her brother's physical traits to her own. Yet despite her bodily foibles, Bailey still loves her, the young Maya says. This points again to the girl's complete embarrassment over her body, which was made so apparent in the prologue and will persist as a weighty albatross throughout the text. Bailey is so wonderful for always taking revenge when others make fun of his sister's looks. Again, this example focuses on her appearance, and, even worse, the young girl cites her own elder relatives as being responsible for the rude comments. Bailey's ability to get back at them shows his cunning and serves as one of the earliest examples in the book of children being smarter, more sensitive, and more virtuous than adults, and knowing it. Bailey is outrageous and exacting and has boundless energy. Yet seldom is he punished, since he is the pride of the family, which the young girl accepts without feeling weakened or in competition. He is so incredible to the lonely Maya that she calls him her "unshakable God."

The chapter switches to covering traditions in the town related to food. At least twice a year Maya and Bailey go into town to buy real meat, with Bailey, of course, being the one to carry the money. Fellow black inhabitants are all greeted along the way, and friends are even briefly visited—there is a notably different atmosphere than the one confronting them on the white side of town. Segregation keeps the children from seeing many white people, which makes Maya never believe that "whites are really real." She does know they must be dreaded, as they live their "alien unlife."

An explanation of Momma's two key commandments— "Thou shall not be dirty" and "Thou shall not be impudent"— opens **chapter five**. Maya and her brother must be clean, even if it requires washing outside on the bitterest nights. Also, they must treat their elders with the utmost respect. Everyone Maya knows follows these rules, except for "powhitetrash children," whom Maya describes as living on Momma's land but still treating her Uncle Willie and Momma not only in the most disrespectful manner but as if they were mere servants. These descriptions smoothly set up the reader for the climactic event of the chapter—Momma's confrontation with young white girls who mock her in an attempt to get her to lose control. Maya describes it as "the most painful and confusing experience I had ever had with my grandmother."

Momma poses a formidable opponent. She sees the girls coming up the street and decides not to turn away but to face them, the whole time remaining steady and singing to herself. The girls mimic and tease and culminate their attempts to unsettle Momma by having one girl wearing a dress but no underwear stand on her head. As the young girl's skirt falls over her face, Momma continues to hum, in complete control as her "apron strings trembled."

Before the girls arrive, Momma has made Maya go inside, and the young granddaughter observes the whole shameful scene through the screen door, wishing Momma were inside with her or had let Maya face the girls on her own. Maya wishes she could shoot the girls, scream, or throw black pepper, or even lye, on them. Yet in the same sentence containing these desires, she remarks, "but I knew I was as clearly imprisoned behind the scene as the actors outside were confined to their roles." She recognizes the deranged societal machine at work. Yet while Maya has burst into tears, Momma sings "Glory,

glory, hallelujah," triumphant, albeit within society's very sick rules. This is an example of Maya's writing fitting into the narrative slave tradition, as many critics have commented. The evil prejudiced system is a part of everyday life, and the author works to find ways to fight it, just as the slave writers did.

In **chapter six**, a sharp portrait is given of Reverend Howard Thomas, a preacher who would visit their Christian Methodist Episcopal Church in Stamps every three months and stay at Momma's house the night before his Sunday sermon. Maya and Bailey despised him, not only because he was ugly and fat but because he never remembered their names, always ate the best chicken parts at their Sunday meal, and droned on and on with his blessing until the food was quite cold.

The family heads off to church on one Sunday when Reverend Thomas is to preach, and in able storyteller fashion, Angelou precedes the description of the event with her recollection of another church occurrence. On that remembered day one churchgoer, Sister Monroe, became so full of the spirit that she ran up to their usual preacher on the pulpit, yelling "Preach it," and inspiring two others to do the same. This resulted in a scuffle, with the reverend and two others down on the altar floor. For weeks after, all Bailey had to do was say "Preach it" and the two children would break into laughter.

This recollection prepares the reader for what could happen on this particular hot day in church, which Angelou returns to describing. She tells us that Momma sits directly in view of the two children, so she can cast them appropriately stern looks as needed to keep them behaving. When Maya looks over to her on this day, though, Momma's watchful eye is on Sister Monroe instead of the children. Sister Monroe's voice quickly becomes loud during the service. A few children try to stifle giggles, and Bailey nudges his sister, saying, "Preach it." While two men try to hold Sister Monroe to prevent another embarrassment, she will not be restrained and rushes once again to the pulpit.

Reverend Thomas, who has heard the story of her previous escapade, immediately starts off the pulpit from the side opposite her, continuing his preaching. While many other churchgoers are following Sister Monroe, she does catch up with the reverend, and hits him on the back of the head with her purse—twice—causing his false teeth to catapult from his mouth and to the floor just next to Maya's shoe. By this time, Maya is consciously holding back laughter, but she cannot manage once she hears laughing snorts emanating from her brother. Reminiscent of the experience related in the prologue, Maya again has lost control in church, but this time she and her brother are in it together. They laugh with complete abandon, slipping off the bench, screaming, and kicking and laughing even louder when they look at each other.

Momma yells to them; Uncle Willie, who is closest, threatens to whip them, and they end up in the parsonage next door being beaten by Uncle Willie. He persists, and they are saved not when a sympathetic churchgoer forces him to stop but when the minister's wife asks him to stop because their cries are interrupting what is left of the service. While at least one critic has written about Momma's religion as one of the strongest influences on Maya's life, apparently it is not necessarily a strong positive influence when in the confines of the church. Instead it is absurdist, not necessarily because of what the church stands for but because the church is composed of people with comical foibles. As will occur at other points in the book, the children see the insanity of the very adults whom they are supposed to respect.

Many critics also have spoken of Angelou's keen skill with humor, working it through her book at key points and using it as a saving grace from the tragedy strewn throughout the work. Angelou uses hope in a similar way, although the hope that Momma has is strongly based on her traditional religious perspective, while Maya's seems to come from another source. Whatever their sources, both humor and hope make the young girl's life livable, when at times it is so very bad. They serve as a wonderful testament to Angelou as well as to the human spirit.

In the very brief **chapter seven**, we are given more insight into Momma, who was married three times but whose spouses remain a mystery to the children. They hear from others in the town that Momma was pretty when she was young, but all that Maya can see in her is her strength. Momma intends to teach Maya and Bailey life's lessons as she and all the blacks before her had learned them. The only lesson stated here is her perspective on how to deal with whites. She believed that one risked one's life if one spoke to a white person and that even in their absence they should not be spoken of harshly. She saw this approach not as cowardly, but realistic.

The attempt to understand whites continues in the beginning of **chapter eight**. While whites are, for the most part, separate from blacks, the children develop a "fear-admiration-contempt" for the whites' cars, houses, children, and women. Maya cannot understand how they can spend money so lavishly. While her grandmother had more money than the poor whites and owned land and houses, she still taught the children to waste nothing. "Of course, I knew God was white too, but no one could have made me believe he was prejudiced," Maya rationalizes. Her child's logic assumes that if the whites are rich, powerful, and beautiful, God must be one of them. Again, she is on the outside.

Once the Depression hits the small town, though, the ability to even consider wasting anything completely vanishes. Momma uses her businesswoman's acumen to keep her poor customers still coming to her store even though many are now struggling financially. Starkly contrasted to this intense trouble is the life Maya hears her parents are living "in a heaven called California, where we were told they could have all the oranges they could eat. And the sun shone all the time. I was sure that wasn't so. I couldn't believe that our mother would laugh and eat oranges in the sunshine without her children." Maya had believed her parents were dead, until one Christmas when the parents sent toys for her and Bailey. The children reacted to the presents by going out in the cold and crying. Now that their parents must be alive, Maya is consumed with wondering why they had sent their own children away, figuring that she and Bailey must have done something terribly wrong.

Bailey tells Maya that if the toys really did come from their parents it might mean that they would be coming to take the children back. Maybe their parents had finally forgiven them for whatever they had done. Both children destroy the doll that was sent but save the tea set, so they will have it when their parents appear. The doll is described in a straightforward way as having blond hair and blue eyes—the exact traits that we learned in the prologue that Maya wishes she had and is so embarrassed to not have. This is only one of the first great pains the parents will cause their children.

The **next chapter** occurs one year later on the day their father appears, just as Bailey anticipated, with seemingly no warning. All of their imaginings of him must now be thrown aside. He is big and "blindingly handsome." Maya is so proud of him and knows he must be rich "and maybe had a castle out in California." But she also has fears that maybe he is not her real father and that she is just an orphan the family had picked up to keep Bailey company. For three weeks their father is the center of attention at the store as people come to see him, and then he announces that he must go back to California. Maya is relieved, until she learns that he is taking her and Bailey with him.

Maya panics and does not know if she should really go. But she ends up squeezed in the back of the car, emotionally and physically uncomfortable. Bailey and their father make jokes in the front, and she is disturbed to realize that Bailey is trying to butter him up. The children then receive their next monumental shock: they are not going to California but to St. Louis to meet their mother. Maya is immediately terrified, fearful that her mother might laugh at them the way their father has or that her mother might have other children living with her now. Maya says she wants to go back to Stamps, cries, and asks Bailey in pig Latin if he thinks that this is their real father or a kidnapper.

St. Louis is described as hot, dirty, and rather ominous. Maya is "struck dumb" by her mother's beauty, which "literally assailed me." Mother wears lipstick, the first sign that this is a very different woman from their grandmother, who had said wearing lipstick was a sin. Mother has an enormous smile, and

Maya surmises that she had sent them away because she was too beautiful to have children. Bailey is immediately in love with her and has forgotten her rejection of them. Their father leaves the children in St. Louis after a few days, and Maya remarks that it hardly mattered either way, since both he and her mother are strangers to her.

This chapter again focuses on physical description. Angelou, the master portrait artist, chooses to focus on surface characteristics—not only because this is always a large part of one's first impression of a person but also because it indicates the child's obsession with her own physicality and how it fits in with the world. Also, it seems fitting that little is said about the father's personality, even after the children have been with him for weeks, because he is, in fact, a man overly concerned with the surface. The quotes showing Maya's immediate reaction to her mother also serve as a foreshadowing of terrible events yet to occur because of their living with their mother.

A more thorough taste of St. Louis and Mother's Baxter family is given to the reader in **chapter ten**. The black section of St. Louis is replete with gambling and other illegal activities, and those who partake of these practices are frequenters of Grandmother Baxter's house, where the children live for their first six months in St. Louis. Grandmother Baxter is a powerful figure in the community because of her six mean offspring and her ability to pull strings with the police. An entourage of crooks request her help and in return provide her with favors. She has a strong marriage with her husband, who lives for his family and actually encourages his grown sons to fight. Mother is the only outgoing sibling, but Maya is fascinated by the men's meanness.

In their new school, Maya and Bailey are shocked that their fellow classmates know so little. The teachers recognize the abilities of the two new children and move them ahead a grade so as not to intimidate their peers. In the year that they attend this school, Maya recalls learning almost nothing. The teachers are more formal, cold, and condescending than they had been in Stamps. The children learn to no longer use the phrase "Yes ma'am," and are told to answer with just "Yes." This is only one example of how the teachings of their grandmother in Arkansas no longer apply in the world of St. Louis.

The children's lives are remarkably different. Instead of being under the steady watchfulness of their Stamps grandmother, here in St. Louis they seldom even see their mother at home. Occasionally she has them meet her in a dark tavern after school, where they watch her dance and sing the blues. The children learn the time step and are required to show their skill at the bar; it is a far cry from the days of reciting the times tables by the pot-bellied stove, yet Maya approaches the task with the same dedication.

After six months, the children move in with their mother and have to adjust yet again. While it is never spoken of, Maya constantly feels the threat that Mother could return them to Stamps if they are disobedient or too troublesome. As a result, the young girl alters her demeanor, making no move without extreme care. Also in this chapter, the reader gains a brief glimpse of Mother's boyfriend, Mr. Freeman, who lives with her. Maya sees him as notably older than her mother and lucky to have her.

Maya tells us in **chapter eleven** that St. Louis is a foreign country that she will never get used to. She does not view it as home. "I carried the same shield that I had used in Stamps: 'I didn't come to stay,'" Angelou writes. This is a flashback to the prologue, where she had to recite these exact words in church. The lines, then, are not just words adults forced her to memorize but words that she views as applicable to her life. Yet whereas the idea of the first line of poetry, which deals with identity and not fitting in, has been recurring throughout the first ten chapters, the relevance of the second line never has been pointedly stated in the book until now. While we have recognized Maya's longing for being accepted and loved in a stable home, this is the first statement telling us that all along she has kept herself from letting her defenses down, from ever allowing herself to believe she really could be home. While the defense helps ease her pain, her desire for a home and love will persist throughout the book and manifest itself in various ways. For example, both Maya and Bailey develop "afflictions."

Bailey stutters, and Maya has terrifying nightmares, causing her mother to sometimes bring the girl into bed with her and Mr. Freeman.

One morning Mother has gotten up early, leaving Maya alone in the bed with Mr. Freeman. He involves the young girl in his masturbation, and she is confused yet feels very comforted when he holds her afterwards. So intense are her needs that she says, "I feel at home," the very feeling she previously has prevented herself from having. It is a poignant scene. "From the way he was holding me," Angelou writes, "I knew he'd never let me go or let anything bad ever happen to me. This was probably my real father and we had found each other at last."

But Mr. Freeman threatens Maya, saying that if she ever tells anyone what happened that morning he will kill Bailey. The young girl is stunned and confused. Angelou writes that she did not dislike Mr. Freeman at this point but "simply didn't understand him." For a brief few weeks, Maya actually wishes he would hold her again. Unwittingly she climbs into his lap, provoking his ejaculation, after which he stops speaking to her for months. She feels lonely and rejected but soon forgets about him and loses herself in books and comic strips. Since Bailey is more distanced from her, the books pose a fantastic escape, and she spends most of her Saturdays at the library, completely undisturbed.

While Maya nearly has forgotten about the sexual incidents with Mr. Freeman, in **chapter twelve** the reader learns that these encounters are not over. This time is different, though. As soon as Maya realizes Mr. Freeman's intentions, she backs away and says no to him, despite the fact that she had liked it when he held her before. This time is also worse because Mr. Freeman rapes the eight-year-old girl and she faints.

Mr. Freeman tells Maya again that she must not tell anyone what has happened. She promises not to and says she must go lie down. Instead, he hands her the soggy underwear that he has rinsed out and sends her off to the library. The child is half delirious, walking down the street and feeling like her hips are coming out of their sockets, and so she returns home and goes to bed. Her mother and Bailey are concerned and assume she is sick, since so many children then have the measles. When they leave Maya's room, Mr. Freeman looms over the girl and again threatens her about not telling anyone. Through the night Maya keeps waking to hear her mother and Mr. Freeman arguing, and she hopes he will not hurt Mother too.

In the morning, Mother tells Maya that Mr. Freeman has moved out, and the young girl wonders whether that means it is safe to tell what really happened to her. She wonders whether Bailey will still love her. She fears she is dying and asks Bailey to take her away to California or France or Chicago. Since she has sweated so much, Mother says they must change the sheets, and this is when they find Maya's stained underwear, which that she has hidden under the mattress.

Chapter thirteen opens with Maya in the hospital and Bailey asking her who hurt her. She explains that she must keep this a secret, since the man will kill Bailey. But when her brother says that he will not let that happen, she, in her child-like innocence, believes him and tells him. He breaks into tears, and Maya starts to cry as well.

Mr. Freeman is arrested, and shortly thereafter Maya testifies against him in an over-crowded courtroom, filled with, among others, Grandmother's thug-like acquaintances. Afraid as the lawyer tries to trip her up, Maya swears to herself that she hears people in the courtroom laughing at her. Then she stiffens in even greater fear when the lawyer asks her whether Mr. Freeman had ever touched her before the day of the supposed rape. If she tells the truth, she believes her uncles will kill her, Grandmother Baxter will stop speaking to her, Mother will be so disappointed, and, worst of all, Bailey will find out that she has kept big secrets from him.

Feeling very pressured, the young Maya lies and says that Mr. Freeman had never touched her before. Immediately upon speaking the words, she feels a lump in her throat as though she cannot breathe. Mr. Freeman is found guilty and sentenced to prison, yet he manages to get released the very same day.

At home later that day, Maya fears she is really in trouble when a policeman comes to the door. She and Bailey hear the man tell their grandmother that Mr. Freeman has been killed. "Poor man," Grandmother whispers, and then she asks whether they know who killed him. She plays the sympathetic role with the policeman, yet the reader, who has already heard about the ruthlessness of the Baxter clan, can guess what has happened.

Angelou draws us immediately back into Maya's thoughts. The young girl is shocked, assuming that because she has lied she is responsible for Mr. Freeman's death. She believes that she will never go to heaven. "Even Christ himself turned His back on Satan. Wouldn't He turn His back on me?" she asks herself. "I could feel the evilness flowing through my body and waiting, pent up, to rush off my tongue if I tried to open my mouth. I clamped my teeth shut, I'd hold it in." The young Maya is horrified and cannot even talk to Bailey about it. He, too, is terrified.

Maya decides right then not to speak again, except to Bailey, for she is convinced that if she does speak, another person may die. This reaction is at first accepted by the family, but when the doctor declares the child healed, everyone expects her to return to her previous self. When she does not, she is called impudent and sullen and then is punished. Yet none of this brings Maya back, and so the occurrence that the children had dreaded from the moment they arrived takes place: they are sent back to Arkansas with her defensive shield up, Angelou claims she does not care about being sent away. She does care very much, however, that her best buddy Bailey is completely distraught over leaving.

"The barrenness of Stamps was exactly what I wanted ... ," Angelou writes in **chapter fourteen**. "Into this cocoon I crept." She appreciates the fact that nothing happens in Stamps and that she no longer has to cope with the free-wheeling St. Louis. The two children now have celebrity status in Stamps. After all, they had been whisked away in a big shiny car by a well-spoken father with a "big-city accent" to a glamorous place and have returned to tell about it. Momma is so proud of them she does not immediately make them responsible for chores. Bailey sops up the limelight, telling tall tales of the height of skyscrapers in

St. Louis, the bounty of their watermelons, and the monstrous depth of their snow. Maya remains mute, not only not emitting sound herself but struggling with letting sounds in as well. Her senses are dulled, and she worries about her sanity. The people of Stamps accept her silence as part of her "tender-hearted" nature, viewing her as overly sensitive and "in delicate health."

Yet upon reading the events in **chapter fifteen**, the reader realizes that Momma knows Maya cannot stay mute forever and that something should be done to help her. At the opening of the chapter, Maya tells us that she remains quiet for nearly a year but then becomes acquainted with a woman "who threw me my first life line." The woman is Mrs. Bertha Flowers, one of the few aristocratic blacks in their town. Before we even find out about how Maya meets this woman, Angelou writes that Mrs. Flowers "was one of the few gentlewomen I have ever known, and has remained throughout my life the measure of what a human can be."

While Mrs. Flowers is so different from Momma, the two have an intimacy that Maya does not understand. Maya is embarrassed when she hears Momma use improper English when speaking to the beautiful, refined woman. The young girl is even more embarrassed when Mrs. Flowers compliments Momma on her sewing. In response, Momma insists on lifting Maya's dress over her head to show the woman that even the stitches on the inside are nearly perfect. Mrs. Flowers realizes Maya's dismay and politely tries to keep Momma from pulling the dress over the young girl's head, yet another sign of the woman's sensitivity and grace.

Maya is told to walk home with Mrs. Flowers and carry her groceries. En route Mrs. Flowers says she knows that Maya's written school work is very good but that the teachers have trouble getting her to talk in class. She says that no one will make her talk but explains that language is what separates man from the lower animals, which gets Maya thinking. Mrs. Flowers also says that she knows the young girl reads a lot, but that it is necessary for the human voice to infuse the written word with deeper meaning. Maya readily soaks this in as well.

Maya is enchanted by the woman's home and the fact that she has made lemonade and cookies just for Maya, and even gives her extras to bring home for her brother. She listens as Mrs. Flowers explains that even though some people have not been fortunate enough to have a formal education, the young girl must realize that some of them are even more intelligent than college professors. Apparently the woman has sensed Maya's embarrassment over her own grandmother. Mrs. Flowers reads aloud to Maya and gives her books to take home, telling her to pick a poem to memorize, so she can recite it at their next visit.

The young girl runs home in a rush of excitement. "I was liked, and what a difference it made. I was respected not as Mrs. Henderson's grandchild or Bailey's sister but for just being Marguerite Johnson," Angelou writes. She is thrilled to have had Mrs. Flowers read to her from her favorite book and make cookies just for her. The identity issues that have posed a major problem for the girl throughout the book so far finally are being chipped away.

Momma hits Maya with a switch upon her return from her visit with Mrs. Flowers because she misunderstands something the girl says, interpreting it as a curse. The incident points out how different the world of Mrs. Flowers is from Momma's world. But the fact that Momma is at least partially responsible for the meeting of Maya and Mrs. Flowers and that she wants her grandchildren to grow up properly show the possibility for a valuable mixing of the two very different worlds. Once again, Angelou proves herself the able designer of her tale, as many critics note, setting up striking contrasts at both the start and end of the chapter.

The rich life of Mrs. Flowers also contrasts that of an upper-class white woman, Mrs. Viola Cullinan, with whom Maya gets a job in **chapter sixteen**, as part of her education about life's "finer touches." Maya is taught by Miss Glory, Mrs. Cullinan's cook, whose slave ancestors had also worked for the rich woman's family. Miss Glory is very patient with Maya, and Maya is fascinated with the novelty of the many pieces of silverware, special dishes and glasses for specific purposes, and many pieces that she had never known existed. She feels sorry for the plump Mrs. Cullinan when she finds out that her husband has had two children with a black woman.

Yet the pity quickly wears away when Mrs. Cullinan's friend suggests she call Maya "Mary," since it is shorter than her full name of Margaret. The next day Mrs. Cullinan does, in fact, take the suggestion and use the name Mary. She explains to Glory that this name is shorter and will be what she uses from now on. Maya is furious and feels no better when Glory tries to calm her by telling her that Mrs. Cullinan shortened her name too and that it actually worked out quite well.

When Maya later discusses the effrontery with Bailey, he devises the perfect stratagem that will not only bring revenge but get Maya out of ever having to go back to Mrs. Cullinan's. The next day Maya carries out the plan. She purposefully drops an empty serving tray. When Mrs. Cullinan yells "Mary!" Maya drops the woman's favorite casserole piece and two of her favorite green glass cups. Mrs. Cullinan falls on the floor, and she begins to cry. When her friend asks her whether "Mary" did this, Mrs. Cullinan yells back, "Her name's Margaret, god-damn it, her name's Margaret!" as she throws a broken piece of plate at Maya. Mrs. Cullinan has learned her lesson, and this is the first time in the book that Maya successfully fights for her dignity. It is notable that the confrontation is caused by the woman's not accepting Maya's name or identity, since developing an identity is one of the strongest concerns in the book.

Yet another of the key concerns in the book is that fear is common not only for the two children but for blacks in general. **Chapter seventeen** opens on a seemingly normal Saturday morning, Maya's favorite day of the week, even though it is filled with a near unending list of chores. Yet the typical day becomes haunting when Bailey does not return from the movies at his usual time and it becomes darker and darker as the family waits for him. Maya feels she has the most to lose if he is found dead, for he is all she has.

Angelou describes the night as "enemy territory" as she and Momma walk with a flashlight to meet Bailey. "The Bluebeards and tigers and Rippers could eat him up before he could scream for help," we are told by the young Maya. Finally Bailey's figure is seen ahead in the dark. When Maya and Momma reach him, he provides no explanation of where he has been and even pushes Maya away as if she is a stranger. She is completely confused and frightened by his lack of response and seemingly overwhelming look of sadness. Upon their return home, Bailey is whipped by Uncle Willie for causing the family grief, and all the while the boy makes no response.

For days Bailey is in his own world. His eyes are vacant; he doesn't speak. Finally he tells Maya that he saw their mother. He explains that he did not really see her but saw a white actress who looked exactly like her on the movie screen. He had stayed so late at the theater the week before because he had to watch the film again. Maya understands why he could not talk to Momma or Uncle Willie about it. "She was never mentioned to anyone because we simply didn't have enough of her to share," Angelou writes, referring to their mother. Months later there is another movie in town featuring the same actress, and this time Maya goes with her brother to see it. It makes her very happy, but it disturbs Bailey deeply again.

Chapter eighteen opens at the end of a weekday at the store, with Maya giving an account of the exhausted field workers. "I thought them all hateful to have allowed themselves to be worked like oxen, and even more shameful to try to pretend that things were not as bad as they were," the young Maya thinks, again disgusted not so much with the black plight as with the black response to it. One worker tells Momma he is going to the revival meeting, and Maya wonders whether her race is full of masochists since the man rightfully should be going home to collapse into bed.

Angelou takes us to the revival meeting, which the young girl finds shocking for being in a tent rather than in a church and for bringing together the very different people from all of the surrounding churches. The minister's sermon is about charity, but more importantly, about what charity is not. It is not about giving someone a job and then expecting the person to bend down in thanks, he says. Nor is it about paying someone for work and then insisting that the worker call the employer "master," nor about asking that he humble and belittle himself. In short, charity is not about the things that the white people do. The assembled have renewed faith from participating in the service; they know that the white people will get what they deserve and that they themselves must manage through the troubles of this world but will live in a blissful eternity. It is unfortunate, though, that so soon after they leave the tent the reality of the current world floods back in.

A temporary victory also occurs in **chapter nineteen** as the black townspeople squeeze into the store to hear the Joe Louis fight on the radio. As we listen to the radio announcer and the blacks in the store, we never hear the name of the person Louis is fighting but do know what is most important—that he is fighting a white man. With every serious blow that Louis takes, we are told, the entire black race suffers as well. The store is tense until the fight ends and Louis wins and keeps his heavyweight champion title. There is a great celebration in the store, complete with Cokes and candy bars, and there is even alcohol out back. Similar to what occurs in the previous chapter, though, this is only a fleeting victory. People who live far from the store stay in town that night because it is not safe "for a Black man and his family to be caught on a lonely country road on a night when Joe Louis had proved we were the strongest people in the world."

A more long-lasting pleasant event is the summer picnic and fish fry in **chapter twenty**. Even here, though, Maya wishes she had a book to read and finds a quiet spot off by herself. Her sanctuary is invaded by another young girl, Louise Kendricks, who is also ten years old and whom Maya had always believed to be the prettiest female in Stamps after Mrs. Flowers. The two girls are of similar spirit; they play creative games away from the others, giggle and laugh uproariously, and become true friends.

In the same chapter, Angelou writes about receiving a request that she become a fellow classmate's valentine, to which she has mixed reactions. The young girl wonders if it could be a joke or whether the classmate has evil intentions. She becomes more disturbed when Louise explains that the writer of the valentine wants her to be "his love." Maya rips the message in half, and each girl shreds her part into little pieces and lets them escape in the wind.

Adults are shown to be foolish, insensitive, and unaware of children's feelings in this chapter and others in the book. In this instance, Maya's teacher reads out loud some valentines and a note from Maya's admirer. Maya realizes from the sincerity of the note that perhaps it was a mistake to have torn up the first one. She decides to say something extra nice to the boy who wrote it when he comes in the store, yet she is continually tongue-tied and eventually he stops noticing her.

Chapter twenty-one shows us Bailey's entry into sexuality, quite a contrast from Maya's experience in the previous chapter. His concern is with the physical aspects, and he rather innocently lures girls into a tent in the backyard. After a few months of this, he meets a sexually advanced girl who is older than he and to whom he becomes most attached. Yet all is not well with this relationship, for whereas before the young girl would do chores around the store now she seldom does. Also, Bailey is taking items from the store, some of the most expensive ones, to satiate her.

Just as Bailey's personality had changed when he first met the girl, when she disappears he is severely affected as well. He loses interest in life and becomes uncommunicative. The children find out later that the girl had run away with a railroad porter but that she had considered Bailey her only friend in Stamps. The events in the two successive chapters clearly point out the siblings' differing reactions to relationships and members of the opposite sex, just as before these chapters we see their disparate reactions to the movie star who looks like their mother. Whereas Bailey has always been the strong one, in both of these instances Maya appears stronger, although in the instance of the valentine, she initially had rejected its sender to avoid any possible pain. For both children, though, at different points silence serves as a coping mechanism.

In **chapter twenty-two** Maya is confronted with another fact of life—death. Angelou displays the still-young Maya's reaction to death as initially based on fear, a belief in ghosts, and her active imagination, which has been fed by an array of literature. On a stormy night when a tornado is threatening, she is reading *Jane Eyre* as Momma cooks and Bailey and Uncle Willie also are reading. She is the first to hear a rattle at the door, and Bailey lets in their neighbor George Taylor, whose wife has died six months ago. Maya fixates on his compelling watery eyes, which harbor a "nothingness." He proceeds to tell the family that his wife spoke to him just the night before and told him she wanted some children. When he says he will tell them exactly what happened, Maya cringes in fearful anticipation of hearing a real ghost story.

Angelou delays the telling of the ghost story and interjects Maya's memory of Mrs. Taylor's funeral, the first one she had ever attended. In listening to the preacher and observing the other funeral attendees, she had come to the grown-up realization that death will come even to her. With this as a backdrop, the young Maya fearfully watches and listens to Mr. Taylor's nightmare. He assures the family that it was not a dream but that it truly happened. He relates how an angel appears to him, laughing, and speaks in the voice of his wife, telling him she wants some children. When they ask him again if it could have been a dream, he is adamant that this really happened. By then Maya is shaking and believes everyone else in the room is as well. Yet Momma responds calmly when Mr. Taylor asks her what this event means, and she gives her realistic, non-supernatural interpretation. Within minutes the room is relieved of the "intoxication of doom" and returns to normal, similar to what happens after other intense experiences described in previous chapters.

Trembling children are again described in **chapter twenty-three**, but at this point the trembling is in anticipation of a great exciting event. Some of the largest classes are graduating from both the elementary school and high school in Stamps, and Maya will be one of the eighth-grade graduates. She has been a top student and will receive special note at the ceremony. In the meantime, she is the center of attention at home and in the store. Her grandmother is working diligently on making her dress, and it is nothing like the dress that she had been so humiliated to wear in the prologue. In fact, this dress and Maya's emotions are very different from what they had been on that day and on most other days described so far in the book. Now her dress is beautiful and makes her look like a sunbeam. "I was going to be lovely," Angelou writes. Even her hair, which she has complained about so many times before, which she had wished was a golden blonde, is now cooperative and pleasing.

Indeed, there is a momentous shift in the chapter. The girl who had been mute, who had thrown up shields in an attempt to prevent herself from emotional harm, is transformed. "The faded beige of former times had been replaced with strong and sure colors," Angelou writes. She has found new happiness; she smiles so much her jaw hurts; she "trammeled memories of slights and insults.... Lost years were pounded to mud and then to dust." Finally, the young girl has hope.

In light of this, it appears quite unfortunate when Maya's graduation ceremony starts with foreboding. The program is changed to accommodate a speaker who is on a tight schedule. He is a white man who lets them know of all the improvements the white school would be receiving. Also, he assures them that he has explained to powerful people that great athletes have come out of their black school. If elected, he will ensure that their school becomes the only black school in that part of Arkansas with a paved playing field. Possibly they could also get new equipment for their home economics and woodshop classes.

As the young children listen, their heads drop in shame and disappointment. Maya says the day is ruined. She is again disgusted at having no control over her life because of her blackness. She hardly can stomach the rest of the ceremony. But then a hush encompasses the room, and the top boy in her class, usually quiet and conservative, leads the class in singing the song that had become known as the Negro national anthem. Parents join in, and the small children who had performed earlier are led back on stage to sing as well. While at other points in the book Maya has remained repulsed by the black situation and blacks' seemingly foolish hope, here there is a great difference. Now she feels a great communal hope and is proud to be black. Unlike other chapters, in which hope disappeared at their ends, here Angelou sustains immense optimism. The transcendence that occurs despite adversity and that is described here and at other points in the work are part of the book's great strength and part of what makes Angelou herself quite astounding.

There is another clash between black and white in **chapter twenty-four**, and again it differs from most of those that have occurred previously. Now Maya has an unbearable toothache, and Momma is ready to fight convention by taking her to see the white dentist in town. He never treats blacks, but Momma believes that since she had lent him money when he was desperate he owes her a favor. At the dentist's back door, Momma and Maya have to wait for over an hour before he will talk to them. Momma is determined to get Maya treatment, yet the doctor will not give in. Finally he makes a horrid comment about blacks and closes the door on Momma and Maya.

But Momma, not ready to give in, makes Maya wait outside as she goes in after the dentist. Angelou gives us Maya's imaginative view of what is taking place. As long as she is given the chance to dream, the young girl dreams big, picturing Momma ordering the dentist out of town by sundown and to never practice dentistry again, as he shakes and cries, helpless before her. On Momma's way out, Maya imagines, she turns the dentist's nurse into a sack of chicken feed. This fantastical victory shows that imagination and storytelling can create escapes from prejudice. The fantasy also hints, according to one critic, that imagination and storytelling can be forms of resisting racism as well.

When Momma does actually come out, she takes Maya on a Greyhound bus to the black dentist. Later we learn the true story of what happened at the white dentist's office. Momma had pushed the dentist enough to get him to give her ten dollars for the bus fare. She had not gotten exactly what she had wanted, but she certainly had not lost either. Even Momma cannot always follow her own advice about steering clear of whites. Maya and the reader get an even greater perspective on Momma's strength and tenacity.

While chapter twenty-four ends with Momma and Uncle Willie laughing over her conquest at the dentist's, **chapter twenty-five** is solemn. Momma announces that she will take the children back to California. Angelou explains that no matter what reason Momma would have given as to why she was planning the trip, the main reason was something that had happened to Bailey. After this ominous introduction, Angelou proceeds to tell us what that was.

Bailey had arrived home one night shaking and unable to speak. This reminds the reader of the earlier chapter when Bailey had been stunned by the movie star that looked like his mother. There, too, the young Maya had been extremely frightened, and the reader wonders if here, too, her anticipatory fear is greater than what the situation may deserve. When Bailey finally talks, he tells his family that he saw a dead, bloated black man pulled out of the pond. The man had been wrapped in a sheet, but a white man yanked it off, grinned, and ordered the black men to take the body into the nearby jail. While Bailey had been watching from a distance, the white man ordered him to help carry the rotting body. Once they got the body inside, the white man pretended he was going to lock in all the men, but then laughed and said it was just a joke when they started to beg him not to do so. The actual prisoners were already yelling that they did not want the body in there with them, and Bailey got out as fast as he could. The young boy asks Uncle Willie and Momma why the whites hate blacks so much, but they seem to have no good answers.

In **chapter twenty-six**, once again we see the startling contrast between the worlds of Momma and the prejudiced South and Mother and her whirlwind beauty. For six months Momma, Bailey, and Maya live in an apartment in California, waiting for their new home to be prepared for them. When Momma leaves, Maya and Bailey realize that once again they are with their beautiful stranger parent. As much as they are on edge, the children end up enraptured by Mother once again, and they realize that she too is nervous as she drives them to an apartment in Oakland where the rest of the Baxters are.

The children go to a school with amenities that their school in Stamps could never have. They are never asked by the family about their schoolwork, and instead of going to church on Sundays, they go to the movies. They find out that Mother's job is playing pinochle for money and running poker games, but she is quick to tell them she never cheats anyone. Also, they learn that only just before their arrival Mother had gotten into a fight with her business partner, with whom she had run a restaurant/casino. The fight had ended with him punching her and her shooting him twice.

Soon after the children's arrival, Mother marries Daddy Clidell, "who turned out to be the first father I would know," Angelou writes. They move with him, a successful businessman, to San Francisco.

Turmoil exists not just in the children's personal lives but in the world at large as well. World War II has started. In **chapter twenty-seven** we are told that in San Francisco the Japanese have disappeared and have been replaced with previously poor Southern blacks, who were recruited to work in the city's shipyards and ammunition plants. Ironically, these factors contribute to making Maya feel like she belongs, for she understands the collective displacement and underlying fear of always being at risk. Even though she is no longer in the South and many of the city's inhabitants believe their city to be unprejudiced, Maya says she knows otherwise. This comment and a short but biting racial story about city-dwellers make us realize Angelou is preparing us for a larger confrontation.

In **chapter twenty-eight** we are given a little more of a taste of what high school is like for Maya. Rather soon after her arrival, she transfers out of a school of brash girls to another outside of the black neighborhood, where initially she is one of only three black students. She feels a connection to the blacks as she rides the streetcars each day to and from school, through the starkly differing neighborhoods. In this new school, though, Maya no longer is one of the smartest students, and most of the other students lack the fear that she has in the classroom. Although Maya is only fourteen, she also gets a scholarship to a college, where she takes drama and dance at night.

Another slice of the underworld is provided in **chapter twenty-nine**, in which Angelou provides a portrait of Daddy Clidell. He is uneducated but successful, owning apartment buildings and, later, pool halls. Maya admires him, and he teaches her an array of card games and introduces her to "the most successful con men in the world." The men proudly explain to her their various tricks against wealthy whites, so she will know better and never be taken by anyone herself.

This chapter serves as a superb prelude to **chapter thirty**, in which Maya has to use her resources and figure the way out of a tough situation. While the previous chapter focused on a surrogate father, chapter thirty brings the young teenager back to her real father, who invites her to spend the summer with him in southern California. She is truly excited, still anticipating that he lives the good life, just as she had when he first drove into Stamps. Yet the illusion is soon destroyed when Maya arrives at her father's rather secluded trailer home, which is also inhabited by his very young girlfriend, Dolores. Maya and Dolores have a near-immediate disliking for each other, and her father seems to takes pleasure in this.

Maya is surprised when her father proposes that just he and she take a trip to Mexico, where he is known to go from time to time, supposedly to pick up food for special dinners. So far Bailey, Sr. has paid her little attention and not attempted to help create a pleasant vacation. Maya is excited by the trip and thinks it will be exotic and fun.

On the way to Mexico, Maya's father stops for some time to drink with a guard, and when he finally gets back in the car he jokingly asks the guard if he wants to marry Maya. While the teenager had wanted to be introduced to her father's friends, she had never envisioned this. The guard starts grabbing her, but eventually her father takes off. They ride along twisted roads to the dirt yard of a bar, where half-naked children are chasing chickens. A group of women emerge, greeting Bailey

Sr. While the women laugh when they hear that Maya is his daughter, once inside the ramshackle building everyone is quite welcoming to both of them. Maya sees her father with new eyes here. He is the center of attention and completely relaxed. Shortly she too is totally at ease, dancing and reveling with complete abandon.

The teenager then realizes she has not seen her father for some time and at first panics at the thought of having been abandoned. When she sees his car outside, she decides to wait there for him, and eventually he appears, thoroughly intoxicated, and falls fast asleep in the car. Rather than spend the night there, Maya decides she will drive them back home, assuming that she has watched enough other people drive to be able to do it herself. The teenager is exhilarated by her success and power as she finally gets the car back to the guard station. At this point she smacks into another car yet still is not afraid, just wondering whether anyone is hurt, whether her father has woken up, and what will happen next.

No one is hurt, and Maya and the passengers of the other car set about waking her snoring father. After some effort, they get him up; he assesses the situation and walks off with his insurance papers, a half-empty bottle of liquor, and the guard and the driver of the other car. In a short time, they return laughing, and Bailey Sr. gets behind the wheel as if completely recovered. Maya is quite angry that he does not praise her for her tenacity and driving, and instead is oblivious to her remarkable accomplishment.

Upon their arrival back at the trailer, in **chapter thirty-one**, Dolores almost immediately starts arguing with Bailey Sr., saying Maya has come between them. The fight escalates until Bailey leaves, slamming the door behind him. While Maya has never liked the woman, she does feel sorry for her, since her father had left Dolores behind to work and worry over what escapades the father and daughter were involved in, and when they would return. Maya decides to console Dolores and feels proud of the decision, which shows what a good-hearted sort she is. Yet the end result is hardly a merciful exchange; it is a physical fight. Dolores calls Maya's mother a whore; Maya slaps her, and Dolores locks her arms around Maya, who finally shoves her away.

Once outside the trailer, Maya realizes there is blood dripping down from her waist. Dolores chases after her with a hammer, and Maya takes refuge in her father's car. Dolores is still screaming wildly when Bailey Sr. and his friends crowd around to calm her. Once she is back in the trailer, the angry Bailey Sr. comes back to get into the car with Maya. She does not warn him about her blood before he sits in the puddle that has made it to the passenger's side; she gets some delight from hoping he will realize that Dolores is quite a monster.

Maya's father takes her to a friend's house to get cleaned up and bandaged, in fear that it would create too much of a scandal to go to a hospital. Afterward, he leaves Maya at another friend's house for the night, meets her in the morning with a perfunctory kiss and a dollar and a half, and says he will be back at the end of the day. Without a plan, Maya packs sandwiches and leaves.

After wandering aimlessly all day, in **chapter thirty-two**, Maya comes to a junkyard and decides to sleep in one of the better-looking cars, feeling quite free in the open air on her own. The next day she meets the other teenage inhabitants of the junkyard, who explain the rules of their make-shift commune. Maya stays with them for a month, learning to drive, curse, and dance. But more important, Maya gains a new security by having been unconditionally accepted by peers of diverse backgrounds. Although there had been much emphasis in the beginning of the book on a need for home and a positive self-image, it takes the experience of being away from adult influence and her various homes for Maya to lose her insecurity. Her self-imposed self-reliance gives her confidence, just as it did when she drove the car with her drunken father. At least one critic has stated that Angelou's search for a home is for a place of acceptance within the self.

Maya calls her mother to get a plane ticket home (**chapter thirty-three**). When Maya arrives in San Francisco, she realizes that it does not seem the same anymore, since she is no longer her naïve young self. We are near the end of the book, and the girl who in the prologue had so wanted to be physically transformed has indeed been transformed, but in a more profound way. She feels not so young anymore, and wiser. And curiously, while her looks have not notably changed, she has become more comfortable with her physical self, after having won a dance contest with another from the junkyard and frequently going out dancing with her brother.

Maya has changed, and her brother is going through his own changes as well. He is not his usual self when she starts to tell him of her exploits in southern California, and he now has hip new friends and is even asserting his independence from their mother. Maya observes the growing confrontations between her mother and Bailey and eventually sees her sixteen-year-old brother take off from home in anger at one o'clock in the morning. When she talks to him the next morning in a dingy rented room a friend has found for him, Maya learns that Mother has not in fact abandoned him. Actually, he is excited to tell Maya that Mother is arranging to get him a job on the railroad. He is confident that he will succeed and work his way up. Not only has he left home but he is taking a job that requires constant travel, perhaps feeling more at home in this instability.

Even though Maya has gained confidence during her summer exploits, she views her brother's optimism as foolhardy. She refrains from telling him so, however, and for once she appears more worldly than he. Angelou had not mentioned Bailey for a few chapters before this, preparing us for this separation. The two siblings who had been inseparable in their early years are intent on finding their own way; for Bailey, this drive is even more powerful than maintaining a close relationship with his sister.

Maya recognizes in **chapter thirty-four** that she is so changed that she cannot go back to living her life the way she had before. Even though she is only fifteen, she decides to leave school and go to work, knowing her mother will admire her gumption, which Mother herself has so much of. Maya decides to get a job as a conductor on the San Francisco streetcars. Despite the fact that her mother tells her there are no blacks working on the cars, Maya decides to fight for the job, showing her again as not just her mother's daughter but as someone who must be her own self. For the most part, in Stamps there were no such opportunities for rebellion—Maya had had the pleasure of breaking her oppressive employer's dishes, but the scheme had been Bailey's and the revenge had been fleeting. Here is Maya's chance to fight and add to her now stronger self-image. She realizes she can have some control over her fate. As critics have commented, this event fits in with the slave narrative tradition, in which a confrontation with the oppressor occurs and there is a drive to achieve order out of chaos.

Maya's confrontation takes the form of daily appearances in the streetcar office, where she asks to see the personnel manager. The teenager not only forgives the clerk she constantly encounters there but sees her as a "fellow victim of the same puppeteer." Maya asks various black organizations and government officials for help in getting the job, but she gets nowhere except to allow them to slightly weaken her resilience and to get her to wonder if she truly is as mad as they believe. What allows her to finally be hired is completely unclear, but Maya does get a job as the first black conductor on the San Francisco streetcars, albeit with seemingly the least-desirable shifts. As she rides the cars proudly, she even realizes she no longer feels secure only in the black areas that they ride through.

Maya keeps the job for one semester and then goes back to school. Again she realizes that she cannot go back, that she is so much wiser and more independent than her fellow classmates. The adult Angelou's voice appears here, commenting on torturous youth. "The command to grow up at once was more bearable than the faceless horror of wavering purpose, which was youth," she writes, preparing us for what is to come in the remainder of the book.

In **chapter thirty-five** we return to the problem of Maya's being unhappy in her body. Now she is concerned not with ugliness but with her lack of femininity, and she jumps to the conclusion that she may be a lesbian. She turns to her mother for help when she feels truly unable to discern whether she is a lesbian, even though she has read about the subject in numerous books. This shows the good comfort level that has grown between them, but when Maya ends up still questioning her sexuality not long after their conversation, we are reminded of the communication problems between the children and adults that seemed rampant in the earlier parts of the book.

We see Maya struggling further with her sexuality and growing up—some of the issues to which critics have suggested gave her book universal appeal. The teenager sets her sights on finding a boyfriend, picks one of the most handsome schoolmates she knows, and offers to have sex with him. She believes this is the only way she can possibly snag a boyfriend, even temporarily.

After her sexual experience, the sixteen-year-old is disappointed that she has not enjoyed it and that it still does not put to rest her concerns that she may not be a normal female. Once again she turns to books, weighing her encounter against what she has read about sex and relationships in novels. In comparison, her experience was sadly lacking. The chapter ends with a one-sentence paragraph that abruptly tells us Maya is pregnant. This is a prime example of Angelou's strength as a storyteller; the surprise ending to the chapter, which is almost the last chapter in the book, compels the reader onward.

Because of the pregnancy, the teenager is consumed with fear, guilt, and self-revulsion, realizing that although for so much of her earlier life she had been like a storm-tossed ship at sea, in this instance she is nearly completely responsible for this "new catastrophe." She turns to Bailey, who has not been mentioned since the chapter in which he left home. He advises her not to tell their mother and Daddy Clidell about the pregnancy, since they will want her to leave school, and Bailey believes it would be nearly impossible for her to go back and get her diploma later. Maya takes Bailey's advice, and the evening that she graduates she writes a note to her mother and Daddy Clidell to tell them the news. They take it in stride, although they are shocked that Maya has kept the secret for so long.

Maya has an easy delivery and admits that "possession

became mixed up with motherhood." One of her overwhelming initial feelings is fear that in her awkwardness she will harm her new son. Mother recognizes this and against Maya's protests has her sleep in her bed with the baby, who is by then three weeks old. Later, when Maya is awakened by her mother, Mother tells her, "See, you don't have to think about doing the right thing. If you're for the right thing, then you do it without thinking." Mother switches the light back off, and Maya pats her baby and returns to sleep. Maya has gone through the adult experience of childbirth without having to think about it. Her mother lessens her fears, and the new mother can rest easy, putting herself in the hands of nature. Again Maya has gone through a monumental human experience while still young, and she has managed fine. We are left with peace, hopefulness, and admiration for this remarkable woman.

SIDONIE ANN SMITH ON ANGELOU'S QUEST FOR SELF-ACCEPTANCE

Two children, sent away to a strange place by estranging parents, cling to each other as they travel by train across the Southwestern United States—and cling to their tag: "'To Whom It May Concern'—that we were Marguerite and Bailey Johnson, Jr., from Long Beach, California, en route to Stamps, Arkansas, c/o Mrs. Annie Henderson" (6). The autobiography of Black America is haunted by these orphans, children beginning life or early finding themselves without parents, sometimes with no one but themselves. They travel through life desperately in search of a home, some place where they can escape the shadow of loneliness, of solitude, of outsiderness. Although Maya and Bailey are travelling toward the home of their grandmother, more important, they are travelling away from the "home" of their parents. Such rejection a child internalizes and translates as a rejection of self: ultimately the loss of home occasions the loss of self-worth. "I'm being sent away because I'm not lovable." The quest for a home therefore is the quest for acceptance, for love, and for the resultant feeling of self-worth. Because Maya Angelou became conscious of her displacement early in life, she began her quest earlier than most of us. Like that of any orphan, that quest is intensely lonely, intensely solitary, making it all the more desperate, immediate, demanding, and making it, above all, an even more estranging process. For the "place" always recedes into the distance, moving with the horizon, and the searcher goes through life merely "passing through" to some place beyond, always beyond. (...)

The undercurrent of social displacement, the fragility of the sense of belonging, are evidenced in the intrusion of white reality. Poor white trash humiliate Momma as she stands erect before them singing a hymn. Uncle Willie hides deep in the potato barrel the night the sheriff warns them that white men ride after black, any black. The white apparition haunts the life of Stamps, Arkansas, always present though not always visible.

Against this apparition the community shores itself up with a subdued hominess, a fundamental faith in fundamental religion, and resignation. The warmth mitigates the need to resist: or rather, the impossibility of resistance is sublimated in the bond of community.

The people of Stamps adapt in the best way they know: according to Momma Henderson—"realistically"—which is to say that they equate talking with whites with risking their lives. If the young girl stands before the church congregation asking, "What you looking at me for?", the whole black community might just as well be standing before the larger white community and asking that same question. Everything had to be low-key: the less looked at, the better, for the black in a white society. High physical visibility meant self-consciousness within the white community. To insure his own survival the black tried not to be looked at, tried to become invisible. Such a necessary response bred an overriding self-criticism and self-depreciation into the black experience. Maya Angelou's diminished sense of self reflected the entire black community's diminished self-image. (...)

One gesture, however, foreshadows Maya's eventual inability to "sit quietly" and is very much an expression of her growing acceptance of her own self-worth. For a short time she works in the house of Mrs. Viola Cullinan, but a short time only, for Mrs. Cullinan, with an easiness that comes from long tradition, assaults her ego by calling her Mary rather than Maya. Such an oversight offered so casually is a most devastating sign of the girl's invisibility. In failing to call her by her name, a symbol of identity and individuality, of uniqueness, Mrs. Cullinan fails to respect her humanity. Maya understands this perfectly and rebels by breaking Mrs. Cullinan's most cherished dish. The girl child is assuming the consciousness of rebellion as the stance necessary for preserving her individuality and affirming her self-worth. Such a stance insures displacement in Stamps, Arkansas.

But now there is yet another move. Once again the train, travelling westward to San Francisco in wartime. Here in this big city everything seems out of place.

> The air of collective displacement, the impermanence of life in wartime and the gauche personalities of the more recent arrivals tended to dissipate my own sense of not belonging. In San Francisco, for the first time, I perceived myself as part of something. (205)

In Stamps the way of life remained rigid, in San Francisco it ran fluid. Maya had been on the move when she entered Stamps and thus could not settle into its rigid way of life. She chose to remain an outsider, and in so doing, chose not to allow her personality to become rigid. The fluidity of the new environment matched the fluidity of her emotional, physical, and psychological life. She could feel in place in an environment where everyone and everything seemed out-of-place.

Even more significant than the total displacement of San Francisco is Maya's trip to Mexico with her father. The older autobiographer, in giving form to her past experience, discovers that this "moment" was central to her process of growth. Maya accompanies her father to a small Mexican town where he proceeds to get obliviously drunk, leaving her with the responsibility of getting them back to Los Angeles. But she has never before driven a car. For the first time, Maya finds herself totally in control of her fate. Such total control contrasts vividly to her earlier recognition in Stamps that she as a Negro had no control over her fate. Here she is alone with that fate. And although the drive culminates in an accident, she triumphs.

This "moment" is succeeded by a month spent in a wrecked car lot scavenging with others like herself. Together these experiences provide her with a knowledge of self-determination and a confirmation of her self-worth. With the assumption of this affirmative knowledge and power, Maya is ready to challenge the unwritten, restrictive social codes of San

Francisco. Mrs. Cullinan's broken dish prefigures the job on the streetcar. Stamps' acquiescence is left far behind in Arkansas as Maya assumes control over her own social destiny and engages in the struggle with life's forces. She has broken out of the rusted bars of her social cage.

STEPHEN BUTTERFIELD ON
I KNOW WHY THE CAGED BIRD SINGS

Ida Wells created the identity of mother and protectress; Maya Angelou in *I Know Why the Caged Bird Sings* (1970) inspires the urge to protect. Her identity is birdlike and vulnerable, the terrified daughter winning her way slowly toward the certainty of motherhood.

In many ways, *I Know Why the Caged Bird Sings* resembles Richard Wright's *Black Boy*. (...)

Maya Angelou's complex sense of humor and compassion for other people's defects, however, endow her work with a different quality of radiance; she does not have Wright's mortal seriousness, or his estrangement, and does not take his risks. Ordinary objects and experiences are rendered with childlike fascination and sensuousness, as though, if they were stones on Jacob's ladder, the reader would be so busy investigating them he would forget to ascend. "The pickle juice made clean streams down his ashy legs, and he jumped with his pockets full of loot and his eyes laughing a 'How about that?' He smelled like a vinegar barrel or a sour angel."[2] Food preparation is described with the loving appreciation of someone to whom good food is a staff of life, and a consummation of meaningful work. (...)

At the same time, food is the center of the child's consciousness, because it is the economic basis of the family's survival; her grandmother earns their living by weighing and measuring flour, selling canned goods, keeping chickens and hogs; when the stock prospers, they prosper; when the food is moving off the shelves and salted into the curing house, the money is coming into the till, and grace to the family table. Feeding hogs, too, is a humorous memory instead of, as in Douglass, a bitter reminder of how little the black children were fed by comparison. (...)

Sloshing down the twilight trails to the pig pens re-creates the sound of the pails, the dusky path, and the coming darkness, while chuckling gently at the "romance" of childhood: she follows the twilight trail, not to see the Wizard, but to slop the hogs. Their gratitude, grunts, and tender pink snouts evoke the kind of feelings one might have about spoon-feeding a hungry baby: the kinship with the hog, the recognition of the animal in ourselves (the children grunt a reply), the sticky mess, our adult fastidiousness, and the creature's total, droll, candid indifference to anything but its own needs. Humor like this is not satire, but love for the sounds and sights of being alive.

This loving attachment to objects, which is also a responsibility to them and insistence on their reality, permeates the style itself in the form of solid images, rooted in the basic rituals of our physical presence: eating, excreting, playing in the dirt, and running barefoot. (...)

But, unlike *Black Boy* and *The Life and Times*, the subject of *I Know Why the Caged Bird Sings* is not really the struggle of the bird; it is the exploration of the cage, the gradual discovery of its boundaries, the loosening of certain bars that she can slip through when the keepers' backs are turned. Wright gave his "whole being" over to coping with the atrocities that surrounded him, and Douglass's principal concern was always the abolition of slavery. For Maya Angelou, resentment of the whites, and the necessity to break through their closed walls of hostility, are forced on her from time to time because she must live in relation to their world; she experiences often the humiliation of their scorn without being able to make an honorable response. But her primary reasons for living, her happiness, sorrows, lessons, meanings, self-confidence, seem to come from within her private circle of light. Part of her is always untouched by the oppression, observing and commenting on it from a distance. What makes the difference may be a closer integration with her background: she never had to defend herself with a knife from the assaults of her family; her mother always maintained a degree of independence, aggressiveness, and beauty that gave Maya a belief in her own powers and a person to consult and emulate when something happened to weaken that belief. The women respected and supported each other. Her grandmother's general store gave the family a position of strength in the black section of Stamps, Arkansas, that was available to few other blacks. The most traumatic experience of her childhood, being raped, has no overt racial content; the rape was committed by a black man, avenged by her uncles, and scarcely involved the white authorities at all.

Note
2. *I Know Why the Caged Bird Sings* (New York: Random House, 1970; rpt. New York: Bantam, 1971), p. 18.

GEORGE E. KENT ON THE UNIQUENESS OF *CAGED BIRD*

In the attempt to define a major strand of development in a black autobiographical tradition, then, I've outlined the theme of a journey through a highly heated chaos deriving from black life's ambiguous relationship to American institutions, an erosion of faith in the American Dream idea which earlier had provided grounds for optimism, and a controversially developing sense of negativity concerning the quality of black life in America.

I Know Why creates a unique place within black autobiographical tradition, not by being "better" than the formidable autobiographical landmarks described, but by its special stance toward the self, the community, and the universe, and by a form exploiting the full measure of imagination necessary to acknowledge both beauty and absurdity.

The emerging self, equipped with imagination, resourcefulness, and a sense of the tenuousness of childhood innocence, attempts to foster itself by crediting the adult world with its own estimate of its god-like status and managing retreats into the autonomy of the childhood world when conflicts develop. Given the black adult's necessity to compromise with prevailing institutions and to develop limited codes through which nobility, strength, and beauty can be registered, the areas where a child's requirements are absolute—love, security, and consistency—quickly reveal the protean character of adult support and a barely concealed, aggressive chaos.

We can divide the adults' resources, as they appear in the autobiography, into two areas of black life: the religious and blues traditions. Grandmother Henderson, of Stamps, Arkansas, represents the religious traditions; Mother Vivian Baxter, more of the blues-street tradition.

Grandmother's religion gives her power to order her being, that of the children, and usually the immediate space surrounding her. The spirit of the religion combined with simple, traditional maxims shapes the course of existence and the rituals of facing up to something called decency. For Maya and her brother Bailey, the first impact of the blues-street tradition is that of instability: at the ages of three and four, respectively, the children are suddenly shipped to Grandmother when the parents break up their "calamitous" marriage. (...)

The confrontation of the self with blues-street tradition takes place while she is with her mother, Vivian Baxter, in St. Louis and California. The author manages the same just balance in portraying it. Because of the different levels of the tradition in which various members of the family are involved, because of the fluid movement some make between it and other traditions, and because of the originality with which the mother's portrait emerges, the exposure is fresh, vivid, lasting. Some of the strict man–woman codes reflected by folk ballads emerge from the character of the mother. Men are able to remain with her only so long as they honor the code, one having been cut and another shot for failure to show proper respect for the mother's prerogatives. In this fast life area of black tradition, the children receive great kindness and considerable impact from built-in instabilities. Mother Vivian is kind in counseling Maya concerning her sexual confusions, in creating a celebrating atmosphere that children would love, in her matter-of-fact acceptance of Maya's unwed motherhood, and in the strong support she gives to the idea of self-reliance and excellence. She herself is the embodiment of bold aggressiveness and self-reliance. (...)

Both children are in inner turmoil over their relationship to their beautiful, tough, and coping mother: Maya because of the paradox involved in being the ungainly and awkward daughter of the beautiful mother; Bailey, her brother, because the instability he is put through increases his oedipal ties to her. Chapter 17 is a poignant statement of Bailey's quest for his mother through a movie screen heroine who resembles her. (...)

Thus the author is able to give a just balance to the qualities of both traditions and to reveal the exact point where the universe becomes absurd. A good deal of the book's universality derives from black life's traditions seeming to mirror, with extraordinary intensity, the root uncertainty in the universe. The conflict with whites, of course, dramatizes uncertainty and absurdity with immediate headline graphicness. What intensifies the universalism still more is the conflict between the sensitive imagination and reality, and the imagination's ability sometimes to overcome. Maya and her brother have their reservoir of absurd miming and laughter, but sometimes the imagination is caught in pathos and chaos, although its values are frequently superior. (...)

The major function of the imagination, however, is to retain a vigorous dialectic between self and society, between the intransigent world and the aspiring self. Through the dialectic, the egos maintain themselves, even where tragic incident triumphs. In a sense, the triumph of circumstance for Maya becomes a temporary halt in a process which is constantly renewed, a fact evident in the poetic language and in the mellowness of the book's confessional form.

Finally, since *I Know Why* keeps its eyes upon the root existential quality of life, it makes its public and political statement largely through generalizing statements which broaden individual characters into types: Grandmother Bailey into the Southern mother; Maya into the young black woman, etc. And the after-rhythms of the American Dream can flow in occasionally without gaining the solemnity of a day in court.

The uniqueness of *I Know Why* arises then from a full imaginative occupation of the rhythms flowing from the primal self in conflict with things as they are, but balanced by the knowledge that the self must find its own order and create its own coherence.

SONDRA O'NEALE ON THE PERCEPTION OF BLACK WOMEN

The Black woman is America's favorite unconfessed symbol. She is the nation's archetype for unwed mothers, welfare checks, and food stamps. Her round, smiling face bordered by the proverbial red bandanna is the requisite sales image for synthetic pancakes and frozen waffles "just like Mammy use to make." Only her knowledgeable smile of expertise can authenticate the flavor of corporately fried chicken. When sciolists have need to politicize reactionary measures, they usually fabricate self-serving perceptions of "universal" Black women: ostensibly trading poverty vouchers for mink-strewn Cadillacs, or hugging domestic accouterments in poses of beneficent penury, or shaking a firm bodice as a prostituting Lilith, who offers the most exquisite forbidden sex—all cosmologically craved images of a remote, ambivalent Mother Earth. Regardless of which polemic prevails, these mirrors of the same perverted icon provide the greatest reservoir of exploitable and subconsciously desired meaning in American culture.

That said, if the larger society does not know who Black women are, only who it wants them to be; if even Black men as scholars and thinkers writing in this century could not "free" the images of Black women in the national psyche, it remained for Black women to accomplish the task themselves. Thus the emergence of Black feminine expression in drama, poetry, and fiction during the seventies was long overdue. Because ebon women occupy so much space on the bottom rung in American polls of economy, opportunity, and Eurocultural measurements of femininity, some of these new writers know that for Black liberation art must do more than serve its own form, that fictional conceptions of depth and integrity are needed to reveal the Black women's identity, and that ethnic women readers are bereft of role models who can inspire a way of escape.

Although Black writers have used autobiography to achieve these ends since the days of slavery, few use the genre today. One who employs only the tools of fiction but not its "make-believe" form to remold these perceptions, one who has made her life her message and whose message to all aspiring Black women is the reconstruction of her experiential "self," is Maya Angelou. With the wide public and critical reception of *I Know Why the Caged Bird Sings* (*C.B.*) in the early seventies, Angelou bridged the gap between life and art, a step that is essential if Black women are to be deservedly credited with the mammoth and creative feat of noneffacing survival. Critics could not dismiss her work as so much "folksy" propaganda because her narrative was held together by controlled techniques of artistic fiction as well as by a historic-sociological study of Black feminine images seldom if ever viewed in American literature.

No Black women in the world of Angelou's books are losers. She is the third generation of brilliantly resourceful females, who conquered oppression's stereotypical maladies without conforming to its expectations of behavior. Thus, reflecting what Western critics are discovering is the focal point of laudable autobiographical literature,[1] the creative thread which weaves Angelou's tapestry is not herself as central subject; it is rather a purposeful composite of a multifaceted "I" who is: (1) an indivisible offspring of those dauntless familial women about whom she writes; (2) an archetypal "self" demonstrating the trials, rejections, and endurances which so many Black women share; and (3) a representative of that collective obsidian army which stepped out of three hundred years of molding history and redirected its own destiny. The process of her autobiography is not a singular statement of individual egotism but an exultant explorative revelation that she *is* because her life is an inextricable part of the misunderstood reality of who Black people and Black women truly are. That "self" is the model which she holds before Black women and that is the unheralded chronicle of actualization which she wants to include in the canon of Black American literature. (...)

In the end, self-education through literature and the arts gave her the additional fortitude and intellectual acumen to be a Baxter-Henderson woman of her own generation.

When the adult Angelou faced the world, the humble requirements of Stamps, Arkansas, the speakeasies of St. Louis, and the shipyard boarding-houses of San Francisco had passed away. Through art she could preserve the tenacious women who survived the crucibles those eras intended but aside from will and determination she could not extract dependable techniques from their experiences. Hence the conclusions of Angelou herself as role model for this present age: if Black women are to "paddle their own canoes" in postindustrial society they must do it through force of intellect.

Notes

Sondra O'Neale, Ph.D., is an assistant professor of African-American literature at Emory University in Atlanta, Georgia. Topics researched in this article are part of her forthcoming book, *Growing in the Light: Aspects of Bildung in Works by Black American Women Writers*, which is a comprehensive study of the unique rites of passage in Black feminine experience.

1. See the 1977 presidential address of the English Association entitled *Autobiography* by Sir Victor Pritchett (London: English Association, 1977); also Lord Butler, *The Difficult Art of Autobiography* (Oxford: Clarendon Press, 1968). The novelistic approach to reportive prose is also explored in John Hellmann's *Fables of Fact: The New Journalism as New Fiction* (Chicago: University of Illinois Press, 1981).

JOANNE M. BRAXTON
ON BLACK AUTOBIOGRAPHY

Maya Angelou's *I Know Why the Caged Bird Sings* (1970) and Anne Moody's *Coming of Age in Mississippi* (1968) appeared at the end of the civil rights movement of the 1960s, and they carry with them the bitter and hard-won fruit of this era. Angelou and Moody know the harsh realities of life in the Deep South in the mid-twentieth century—in Arkansas and Mississippi, respectively. As the critic Roger Rosenblatt has asserted, "No black American author has ever felt the need to invent a nightmare to make [her] point." As Maya Angelou writes of her childhood: "High spots in Stamps were usually negative: droughts, floods, lynchings and deaths." Touched by the powerful effects of these destructive forces, Maya Angelou and Ann Moody hold themselves together with dignity and self-respect. They move forward toward a goal of self-sufficiency, combining a consciousness of self, an awareness of the political realities of black life in the South, and an appreciation of the responsibility that such an awareness implies. For this chapter, I have selected *I Know Why the Caged Bird Sings* as representative of autobiographies written by black women in the post-civil rights era.

In the Arkansas South of Maya Angelou's childhood, recognized patterns of etiquette between the races asserted white superiority and black inferiority. This etiquette served as a form of social control that pervaded the daily experiences of blacks, who negotiated narrow paths of safety? (...)

Throughout the course of *Caged Bird*, Maya Angelou moves toward this same realism, which is not only a practical political philosophy but also one of the dominant modes of the autobiography. *I Know Why the Caged Bird Sings* distills the essence of the autobiographical impulse into lyric imagery touched by poignant realism. Angelou once said, "I speak to the black experience, but I am always talking about the human condition—about what we can endure, dream, fail at, and still survive." In this spirit, she faithfully depicts her home ground as a version of the universal human experience. (...)

I Know Why the Caged Bird Sings treats themes that are traditional in autobiography by black American women. These include the importance of the family and the nurturing and rearing of one's children, as well as the quest for self-sufficiency, self-reliance, personal dignity, and self-definition. Like Ida B. Wells, Maya Angelou celebrates black motherhood and speaks out against racial injustice; but unlike Wells, she does so from a unified point of view and in a more coherent form. This derives, in part, from Wells's identity as a public figure and Angelou's identity as an artist. As a creative autobiographer, Angelou may focus entirely on the inner spaces of her emotional and personal life. In *I Know Why the Caged Bird Sings*, the mature woman looks back on her bittersweet childhood, and her authorial voice retains the power of the child's vision. The child's point of view governs Angelou's principle of selection. When the mature narrator steps in, her tone is purely personal, so it does not seem unusual that Angelou feels compelled to explore aspects of her coming of age that Ida B. Wells (and Zora Neale Hurston) chose to omit.

Here emerges the fully developed black female autobiographical form that began to mature in the 1940s and 1950s. Like Zora Neale Hurston and Era Bell Thompson, Maya Angelou employs rhythmic language, lyrically suspended moments of consciousness, and detailed portraiture. Her use of folklore and humor help to augment the effect she creates as tale-teller *par excellence*. Maya Angelou takes the genre of autobiography to the heights that Zora Neale Hurston took the novel in *Their Eyes Were Watching God*. If *I Know Why the Caged Bird Sings* reads like a novel, it carries the ring of truth. Speaking in terms of its literary merits, it is perhaps the most aesthetically satisfying autobiography written by a black woman in this period. (...)

The use of portraiture and the feeling of being close to nature and the land contribute to the lyric sensibility of *Caged Bird*, but unlike the earlier autobiographies by Thompson and Hurston, *Caged Bird* admits harsh and painful aspects of the southern black experience before the civil rights era—the economic oppression and racial violence that Thompson and Hurston either knew little about or chose to ignore. This awareness lends Angelou's lyric imagery the knife-sharp edge of realism, something contributed to black female auto-biographical tradition through the Richard Wright school of the 1940s and 1950s. Thematic and structural similarities between the autobiographies of Wright and Angelou result from their common descent from the slave narrative and from the influence of Russian writers, which both read. Another common denominator between Wright and Angelou concerns their view of the "Great Migration," of which both were a part. They depict themselves as participants in a vast historical drama—the movement of rural blacks from the Deep South to the urban centers of the North, hoping to improve their economic and social horizons by escaping the racism and exploitation of the South. Although Wright's tone seems more political than Angelou's, they respond to the same historic moment.

FRANÇOISE LIONNET
ON AUTOBIOGRAPHY AS LITERATURE

The story, though allegorical, is also historical; ... and it is as reasonable to represent one kind of imprisonment by another, as it is to represent anything that really exists by that which exists not.

—Daniel Defoe, *Robinson Crusoe's Preface*

My books. They had been my elevators out of the midden.
                    —Maya Angelou, *Gather Together in My Name*

As a literary foremother, Zora Neale Hurston meant a great deal to Maya Angelou the autobiographer. Urged by her editor to start work on a multivolume project about her life, Hurston said that she really did not *"want"* to write an autobiography, admitting that "it is too hard to reveal one's inner self." Like Hurston, Angelou affirms that she "really got roped into writing *The Caged Bird*," challenged by an editor who dared her to succeed in the difficult task of writing "an autobiography as literature."[1] That she wrote it *as literature* is the specific aspect of her work on which I shall focus in this chapter. Because the autobiographical project was a response to external pressures, it is in many ways directed to a white audience, but at the same time, it succeeds in gesturing toward the black community, which shares a long tradition among oppressed peoples of understanding duplicitous uses of language for survival. Thus a passage of *I Know Why the Caged Bird Sings* encapsulates the questions of "truth" and referentiality as well as Angelou's problematic sense of audience. In that passage, Angelou alludes to her grandmother's secretive and cautious ways with language:

> Knowing Momma, I knew that I never knew Momma. Her African-bush secretiveness and suspiciousness had been compounded by slavery and confirmed by centuries of promises made and promises broken. We have a saying among Black Americans which describes Momma's caution. "If you ask a Negro where he's been, he'll tell you where he's going." To understand this important information, it is necessary to know who uses this *tactic* and on whom it works. *If an unaware person* is told a part of the truth (it is imperative that the answer embody truth), he is satisfied that his query has been answered. *If an aware person (one who himself uses the stratagem)* is given an answer which is truthful but bears only slightly if at all on the question, he knows that the information he seeks is

of a private nature and will not be handed to him willingly. Thus direct denial, lying and the revelation of personal affairs are avoided. [164–65; my italics]

For Momma, the "signifying" of truths and untruths varies according to the status of her interlocutors, and it is in this differentiation between the "unaware" interlocutor and the "aware" that we can begin to understand Angelou's conception of "autobiographical" narration and the double audience she addresses in her writings: an audience split along racial and gender lines but also—and this is the important point here—split between those interlocutors, on the one hand, who share with the narrator an unquestioned sense of community and those, on the other hand, who have a relationship of power over that narrator.

Clearly, for Angelou, writing an autobiography has little to do with "the revelation of personal affairs," and like Hurston, she does not "reveal [her] inner self." Indeed, the passage about Momma can be read as an important example of the "self-situating" power of literary texts.[2] Momma's caution functions as an explicit warning to the reader, who is thus challenged to take note of the double-voiced nature of Angelou's text. Her narrator alternates between a constative and a performative use of language, simultaneously addressing a white and a black audience, "image making" (*CT* 1) and instructing, using allegory to talk about history and myths to refer to reality, thus undermining the institutions that generate this alienated form of consciousness. Here, Angelou provides us with a model for reading and interpreting her narratives, just as Hurston had in her discussions of form and content, truth and hyperbole.

But unlike Hurston, whom we could see as strongly connected to other women in a network of friendly relationships, as well as to rich and solid folk traditions she helps to reclaim—that of "conjure women,"[3] for example—Angelou's narrator is a much more picaresque heroine, a modern-day Moll Flanders, who learns to survive by her wits. In that respect, she too is related to a black folk tradition, but one that is perhaps perceived as more "male": the shiftless trickster or con man, who relies on his ability to tell a good "story" to get out of sticky situations (Brer Rabbit, for instance). The narrator's mother also fits into this tradition. (...)

In this chapter, while focusing on Angelou's double-voiced technique of storytelling, I would like to emphasize three points. The chapter's first section shows how the narrator's love of books, always and everywhere, manages to pull her "out of the midden" (*GT* 90). As Tzvetan Todorov has said, "The desire to write does not come from life but from other writings."[5] Books are Angelou's "first life line" after the traumatic events of her childhood (*IK* 77) and will continue to inspire her throughout her career.[6] During her travels, for example, it is often through the prism of literature that she discovers and appreciates the peoples and places she visits: Verona through Shakespeare, Paris through Maupassant, London through Dickens. It thus seems appropriate, when analyzing her text, to use the literary paradigms she so cleverly manipulates. My second point concerns her use of the religious tradition: she inverts its messages, creating in the process nothing less than a feminist response to Augustine's *Confessions*. Finally, the third section shows how her problematic sense of audience is translated textually by an astute use of various embedded instances of alienated and nonalienated forms of human communication deriving from her folk traditions.

Notes

1. Maya Angelou, interview with Claudia Tate in *Black Women Writers at Work* (New York: Continuum, 1983), pp. 2, 6, hereinafter CT; Robert Hemenway, *Zora Neale Hurston: A Literary Biography* (Urbana: University of Illinois Press, 1980), pp. 275, 278. I shall be using the following editions and abbreviations of Angelou's works: *I Know Why the Caged Bird Sings* (New York: Random House, 1970): *IK*; *Gather Together in My Name* (New York: Random House, 1974): *GT*; *Singin' and Swingin' and Gettin' Merry like Christmas* (New York: Random House, 1976): *SS*; and *The Heart of a Woman* (New York: Random House, 1981): *HW*. This chapter was written before the publication of *All God's Children Need Traveling Shoes* (New York: Random House, 1986).

2. See Ross Chambers, "An Address in the Country: Mallarmé and the Kinds of Literary Context," *French Forum* 11 (May 1986), 199–215 (199).

3. For an excellent study of the "conjure" folk tradition in black women writers, see *Conjuring: Black Women, Fiction, and the Literary Tradition*, ed. Marjorie Pryse and Hortense I. Spillers (Bloomington: Indiana University Press, 1985).

5. Tzvetan Todorov, *Literature and Its Theorists: A Personal View of Twentieth-Century Criticism*, trans. Catherine Porter (Ithaca: Cornell University Press, 1987), p. 165.

6. Scanning the text for overt or covert references to well-known authors or fictional characters, I arbitrarily stopped counting at 100 at the end of the third volume, and I am not including in that figure the many folk poems, spirituals, composers, and songwriters also mentioned.

DOLLY A. MCPHERSON ON ANGELOU'S USE OF COMIC IRONY

While it is true that the content of most Black auto-biographies protest against social conditions, legal restrictions, and cultural tradition that have hindered Blacks, most often Black autobiographers achieve an effect of celebration in protest and affirmation in negation by describing the painful aspects of their experiences with humor and irony. For example, Angelou's use of comic irony is one of the effective techniques of this tradition: Sister Monroe's "spiritual" assault on the minister in *Caged Bird*, Angelou's stylish but inappropriate "get up" for her train trip from San Francisco to Los Angeles in *Gather Together*, the larger-than-life personalities who people her world in *Singin' and Swingin'*, the marvelously comic scene in *Heart of a Woman* in which her South African husband Vus Make chases Angelou around the lobby and up and down the elevators of a ritzy East Side New York hotel, and her leavening account in *Travelling Shoes* of the time she hires an African beautician to braid her hair "Ghanaian fashion," and the woman gives her a style similar to that worn by "pickaninnies" which Angelou mistakenly believes the beautician has done to teach her a lesson on the foolishness of trying to go native. Angelou's irony is not always derisive, as in her description of Mrs. Cullinan or her recapturing of the Mr. Red Leg's tale in *Caged Bird*. More often, as in *Gather Together, Singin' and Swingin', Heart of a Woman*, and *Travelling Shoes*, she turns an irony of love and admiration on Black people with great effectiveness. The five volumes of the autobiography offer numerous excellent examples of Angelou's skillful use of comic irony in describing her relationships with people. A sympathetic irony in dealing with other Blacks has characterized some of the most outstanding work in the Black American literary tradition from Douglass' *Narrative*, to Ralph Ellison's *Invisible Man* and the work of more recent Black writers like William Melvin Kelley, Ishmael Reed, Toni Cade Bambara, and Toni Morrison.

However, Angelou's effective use of self-parody is something new in Black autobiography and, thus, creates a unique place in Black autobiographical tradition. Through numerous excellent examples of self-parody, in the first four volumes particularly, Angelou reveals her youthful silliness, her loneliness, her pretensions, her aspirations, and her instability. While most people encounter life, learn from experiences, and assume a more or less fixed set of postures toward reality, Angelou is unable to settle into security—not merely because life forces her to assume various roles, not merely because life whirls her along, but because, like the picaresque heroine, she is simply unable to keep to a set course. Angelou constantly lets go of the outer stability she sometimes finds because of the need for a vital tension between stability and instability. From the perspective of adulthood, she is able to parody this quality in her younger self for the purpose of analyzing that self. In doing so, she affirms the redemptive potential of all experience and the capacity of the individual human life to create meaning in the face of immense odds. Through the careful selection of actions and attitudes that lend to self-parody, Angelou is also able to reveal the genesis of her character and personality as she views her growth from the perch of adulthood.

Yet nothing in Angelou's prose—not even the parody of self—is merely humorous for the sake of laughter. Behind the laughter is a vision of human weakness, an empathy for people's foibles and their efforts to retain some semblance of dignity in the midst of the ridiculous. One of the values of Angelou's autobiography is to be found in the fact that from *Caged Bird* to *Travelling Shoes*, through all of the experiences recreated and the observations recorded, the work remains both sensitive and poised, humorous and empathetic, realistic and unembittered. How an understanding of the self leads to a feeling of kinship with humankind is excellently demonstrated in Angelou's autobiographical prose, particularly through her skillful use of comic irony and self-parody.

MARY VERMILLION ON ANGELOU'S REPRESENTATION OF RAPE

Important differences obviously exist between [Harriet] Jacobs's antebellum autobiography [*Incidents in the Life of a Slave Girl*] and Maya Angelou's twentieth-century record of her rape at age eight in *I Know Why the Caged Bird Sings* (1969). One important difference is the way in which somatophobia manifests itself in their texts. Because Angelou does not have to contend with the nineteenth-century patriarchal ideology of "true womanhood," she is freer to portray her rape, her body, and her sexuality. Yet Jacobs describes herself as beautiful and sexually desirable, while Angelou, as a child and young adult, sees herself as ugly. Jacobs posits somatophobia outside herself and critiques it as part of slaveholding culture, while Angelou portrays her younger self internalizing and finally challenging the somatophobia inherent in twentieth-century racist conceptions of the black female body. Despite these differences, Angelou's text contains reembodying strategies similar to those of Jacobs. Both women contest somatophobia by questioning religious ideologies, rewriting white literary traditions, and celebrating their bodies and motherhood as symbols of their political struggles. In order to challenge racist stereotypes that associate black women with illicit sexuality, both writers obscure their corporeality in the early part of their texts by transforming the suffering connected with rape into a metaphor for the suffering of their race. In Jacobs's text rape is a metaphor for the severed body and will of the slave, and Angelou similarly uses her rapist's violation of her body and will to explore the oppression of her black community.

Angelou first connects her rape with the suffering of the poor. "The act of rape on an eight-year-old body," she writes, "is a matter of the needle giving because the camel can't."[28] In this description, Angelou subtly links her rapist with the wealthy man whom Jesus warned would have a difficult time getting into heaven, and she reinforces this link by alluding to Jesus's words in her ironic description of a black revival congregation's sentiments: "The Lord loved the poor and hated those cast high in the world. Hadn't He Himself said it would be easier for a camel to go through the eye of a needle than for a rich man to enter heaven?" (108). As she continues to imagine the congregation's thoughts, Angelou makes the connection between her rape and the plight of the poor in class society more racially explicit, and, like Jacobs, she also demonstrates that privileging a future world over the present perpetuates black oppression:

They [the congregation] basked in the righteousness of the poor and the exclusiveness of the downtrodden. Let the whitefolks have their money and power and segregation and sarcasm and big houses and schools and lawns like carpets, and books, and mostly—mostly—let them have their whiteness. (110)

With the image of the camel and the needle, Angelou transforms her rape into a symbol of the racism and somatophobia that afflict Maya and her race throughout much of *Caged Bird*.

Rape in Angelou's text, however, primarily represents the black girl's difficulties in controlling, understanding, and respecting both her body and her words in a somatophobic society that sees "sweet little white girls" as "everybody's dream of what was right with the world" (1). Angelou connects white definitions of beauty with rape by linking Maya's rape with her first sight of her mother, Vivian Baxter. Angelou's description of Vivian echoes that of the ghost-like whites who baffle young Maya. Vivian has "even white teeth and her fresh-butter color looked see-through clean" (49). Maya and her brother, Bailey, later determine that Vivian resembles a white movie star. Angelou writes that her mother's beauty "literally assailed" Maya and twice observes that she was "struck dumb" (49–50). This assault by her mother's beauty anticipates the physical assault by Mr. Freeman, her mother's boyfriend, and Maya's muteness upon meeting her mother foreshadows her silence after the rape. With this parallel Angelou indicates that both rape and the dominant white culture's definitions of beauty disempower the black woman's body and self-expression.

Angelou further demonstrates the intimate connection between the violation of Maya's body and the devaluation of her words by depicting her self-imposed silence after Freeman's rape trial. Freeman's pleading looks in the courtroom, along with Maya's own shame, compel her to lie, and after she learns that her uncles have murdered Freeman, she believes that her courtroom lie is responsible for his death. Angelou describes the emotions that silence Maya:

> I could feel the evilness flowing through my body and waiting, pent up, to rush off my tongue if I tried to open my mouth. I clamped my teeth shut, I'd hold it in. If it escaped, wouldn't it flood the world and all the innocent people? (72)

Angelou's use of flood imagery in this crucial passage enables her to link Maya's inability to control her body and her words. Throughout the text Maya's failure to keep her bodily functions "pent up" signals the domination of her body by others. The autobiography's opening scene merges her inability to control her appearance, words, and bodily functions.

Note

28. Maya Angelou, *I Know Why the Caged Bird Sings* (New York: Bantam, 1969) 65. Future references to this text will be inserted parenthetically. I will refer to the author of *Caged Bird* as Angelou, and to the actor within it as Maya. In my reading of the early part of Angelou's autobiography, I am indebted to Sidonie Smith's discussion of Maya's quest after her "self-accepted black womanhood," to Liliane K. Arensberg's analysis of Maya's dependence on books, and to Francoise Lionnet's exploration of how Angelou makes her body the source and model of her creativity. See Smith, "The Song of the Caged Bird: Maya Angelou's Quest for Self-Acceptance," *Southern Humanities Review* 7 (1973): 365–75; Arensberg, "Death as Metaphor of Self in *I Know Why the Caged Bird Sings*," *CLA* 20 (1970): 275–76; Lionnet, *Autobiographical Voices: Race, Gender, Self Portraiture* (Ithaca: Cornell UP, 1989) 130–68. I differ from these readers in that I discuss the somatophobia and racism in white literary discourse as significant obstacles that Maya must overcome before she can begin to recover from her rape and take pride in her body.

PIERRE A. WALKER ON FORMS OF RESISTANCE

Because chapters eighteen and nineteen explore the limits to subtle, but passive, resistance, the book has to go on to present other possible ways of responding to white oppression. The climactic response, one that consists of active resistance and outright protest, is Maya's persisting and breaking the color line of the San Francisco streetcar company, described in the thirty-fourth chapter. Since *Caged Bird* was written in the late sixties, at the height of the black power movement, and at a time that was still debating the value of Martin Luther King's belief in nonviolent protest, it is no surprise that this act of protest is the climactic moment of resistance to white oppression in the book, a moment that says: Momma's type of resistance was fine in its time and place, but now it is time for some real action.[14] There are at least three other episodes in the second half of *Caged Bird*, however, which explore the line between subtle but passive resistance and active, open protest: the graduation scene (chapter twenty-three), the dentist scene (chapter twenty-four), and the story Daddy Clidell's friend, Red Leg, tells of double-crossing a white con man (chapter twenty-nine).

Falling as they do between the Joe Louis chapter and the San Francisco streetcar company chapter, these three episodes chart the transition from subtle resistance to active protest. The graduation scene for the most part follows the early, entirely positive examples of subtle resistance in *Caged Bird*. The only difference is that the resistance is no longer so subtle and that it specifically takes the form of poetry, which in itself valorizes the African-American literary tradition as a source for resisting white racist oppression. (...)

The primary difference in the graduation chapter is that because the audience sings together, the resistance is a community action. The resistance is still not exactly an outright protest and it still avoids open confrontation, since the white insulter has left and does not hear the singing. Otherwise, the scene resembles a civil rights protest two decades later. The graduation also serves as an introduction for the dentist chapter, which is similar to the graduation chapter because of the way it highlights literature as a possible source for resisting racist oppression, and which is the crucial transitional chapter from subtle resistance to active protest because it opens the door to the eventuality of open confrontation by presenting the closest instance in the book of a black person in Stamps openly confronting a racist white.

The insult in the dentist chapter occurs when Stamps's white and only dentist—to whom Maya's grandmother had lent money, interest-free and as a favor—refuses to treat Maya's excruciating toothache, telling Maya and Momma, "My policy is I'd rather stick my hand in a dog's mouth than in a nigger's" (160). From this point on, though, the chapter ceases to follow the pattern of the previous examples of resistance. Instead, Momma leaves Maya in the alley behind the dentist's office, and in a passage printed in italics, enters the office transformed into a superwoman, and threatens to run the now-trembling dentist out of town. Readers quickly perceive that this passage is italicized because it is Maya's fantasy, but they do have to read a few sentences of the fantasy before realizing it. The chapter ends, after Maya and Momma travel to the black dentist in Texarkana, with Angelou's explanation of what really happened inside the white dentist's office—Momma collected interest on her loan to the dentist, which pays the bus fare to Texarkana—and Angelou's remark: "I preferred, much preferred, my version" (164).

The fantasy scene bears attention because it is the only one like it in *Caged Bird*. It is the only italicized passage in the book and the only one that confuses the reader—even if only for a moment—over what is real and what is fantasy. Some critics have argued that this passage serves the purpose of underlining how limited Momma's ability to fight racism is,[15] and it is true that in a better world, Momma would have been able to exact proper and courteous care from a dentist who was beholden to her. This reading, however, does not account for either the uniqueness of the presentation of the passage or the very real pride Maya feels for her grandmother as they ride the bus between Stamps and Texarkana: "I was so proud of being her granddaughter and sure that some of her magic must have come down to me" (162–63). On the one hand, the italicized passage does highlight the contrast between what Maya wishes her grandmother could do to a racist with what little she can do, thus again demonstrating the limitations of subtle resistance as an overall strategy for responding to racist oppression. On the other hand, the fantasy passage anticipates the kind of outright confrontations between oppressed black and racist oppressor that occurred when Maya broke the streetcar company's color line and in the civil rights movement. Although it is only a fantasy, it is the first instance in *Caged Bird* of a black person openly confronting a racist white, and thus is the first hint that such confrontation is a possibility.

The fact that the fantasy passage is an act of imagination is also significant, since it hints that imagination and storytelling can be forms of resisting racism. It is natural to read the fantasy passage in this way because of its placement immediately after the apostrophe to "Black known and unknown poets" at the end of the graduation chapter (156). Because of this passage praising black poets, we are all the more inclined to see the imagined, italicized, fantasy passage five pages later as itself an instance of poetry. For one, the apostrophe includes in the category of "poets" anyone who uses the power of the word—"include preachers, musicians and blues singers" (156). Thus, anyone who uses language to describe pain and suffering and their causes (i.e., blues singers) belongs in the category of poets. According to this definition, the author of *I Know Why the Caged Bird Sings* is a blues singer, and therefore a poet, too, since telling why the caged bird sings is an instance of describing pain and suffering and their causes, an instance of the blues. Loosely defined, poetry is also an act of imagination, and thus the italicized fantasy passage in the dentist chapter is poetic, since it is an act of imagination. In fact, it is the first instance of Maya being a poet, and thus the first step towards the far more monumental act of writing *I Know Why the Caged Bird Sings* itself. Poetry, in all its forms, can be an act of resistance. The graduation chapter has already made that clear, but the dentist chapter makes it clear that the victim of racial oppression can herself become a poet and use *her* poetry as a form of resistance. Maya had begun to learn the positive power of poetry and of words in the Mrs. Flowers chapter. Now she begins the process of harnessing the power of words to positive effect, a process that concludes with the composition almost thirty years later of the very book in hand.

Notes

14. Angelou has spoken in at least two interviews of the importance of protest in her work ("*Zelo* interviews Maya Angelou" 167; "The Maya Character" 198).

15. See, for example, Neubauer (118). Mary Jane Lupton also feels that in the dentist episode "the grandmother has been defeated and humiliated, her only reward a mere ten dollars in interest for a loan she had made to the dentist" (261).

LYMAN B. HAGEN ON DEPICTIONS OF LOVE

The Angelou descriptive style has been called sensuous. This perhaps reflects her show business experience as a performer. She is keenly aware of emotional impact and demonstrates a tremendous bonding with her readers and listeners. Her style carries great emotional appeal. Angelou's public appearances captivate with words and delivery, and her writing follows this pattern of word awareness and tonal inflection. As noted before, there is a musical lilt to her sentences.

Angelou's treatment of love must be examined in any analysis of her work. There needs to be consideration given to the undercurrent of four kinds of love woven throughout her narratives and her poetry. These perspectives are integral to her content.

Many of Angelou's messages arise from spiritual love. In her twenties, Angelou examined Christian Science and inquired about Judaism, but the pull of the charismatic Christian teaching of her early years was always strong. She never rejected Christianity nor formally severed ties with the Christian Methodist Episcopal Church. This was her early anchor, and it was here that her Bible-quoting "Momma" Henderson held a prominent place. Angelou accepted the existence of a higher being and rejected her first husband's atheistic stance. Angelou was adamant about not wanting her son growing up in a "godless" family. She writes how church attendance made her feel cleansed and whole. The existence of God was a given, as was her love his word. She later found a similar spiritual love amongst her African brothers and sisters. To this day Angelou is actively and unabashedly involved in her religion as she acknowledges publicly. She credits it as being a great source of strength and a linchpin of her philosophy of life.

Angelou also candidly discusses conjugal love. She is proud that she respected and honored the vows of marriage and did not pursue married men. In her marriage to Tosh Angelos, she speaks of physical passion and the general loving relationship they had until they separated. She descries a number of other loving monogamous relationships—emotional and physical—that she had over the years. In one of her poems, she reflects poetically her admiration of a husband. Her poetry includes a number of frank "love poems." She frequently mentions tender responses between couples she knows. She does not confuse love with sex and praises sincere relationships.

Genuine brotherly or familial love, a third type, exemplifies Angelou's love for her brother, Bailey; and for her mother, grandmother, and Uncle Willie, and their love of her. Her grandmother's and mother's love were unconditional, the kind of love she admired in her poem "The Mothering Blackness." The total, fierce, unquestioning love of Angelou for her son is her ultimate expression of this love. Her love for the writer activist Julian Mayfield was deep and strong, and in no way erotic. Angelou said that a black woman, because of economic and other pressures, needs a brother to tell her when she strays from the accepted norm, and Mayfield fulfilled this need. Her poems about freedom fighters are additional expressions of love and admiration. Her books are filled with characters who exhibit unselfish consideration and love of her and each other.

Finally, there is Eros, sexual love, love without emotional content. Sexual love can exist in marriage as well as can conjugal love, but is generally taken to be outside the marital state. Throughout her books she sprinkles references to purely physical encounters, her own and others. She offers no judgment of these relationships. They are accepted as natural occurrences and are not subject to moralistic preaching. The satisfaction of a human need to feel loved, even briefly, is regarded as very basic to mankind.

MARION M. TANGUM AND MARJORIE SMELSTOR ON THE ACT OF GAZING

From the first page of *Caged Bird*, too, Angelou offers a tantalizing invitation into her self—and then as promptly distances us from sharing that personal, all-of-a-sudden incommunicable, experience. This invitation to us to come in and gaze, then that sudden refusal to give us eye contact, is a process that recurs throughout the work. "What you looking at me for? I didn't come to stay ..." (1). With these opening lines, the autobiography establishes a motif of gazing: willing members of the congregation of the Colored Methodist Episcopal Church, and readers who are willing, share a gaze with the young Angelou as she struggles to remember her memorized poem. Resembling the passages that appear in *Let Us Now Praise Famous Men* that Olin describes as incorporating three individuals—author, subject, reader—this direct invitation "takes the reader by the arm, exhorting 'you' to direct your gaze toward a photographed person" (105). But Olin warns that such an invitation is accepted at a price: "You are not going to be able to look 'this terrific thing in the eyes' unless you do so 'with all the summoning of heart you have'" (105). Gazing longer into the eyes of the child Angelou, as the author thrusts before us a repetition of the opening lines, we begin to grasp Olin's warning. Dolly McPherson has noted the importance of the opening lines in pointing to the importance of "something to look at" and has further suggested that since the persona is reciting an Easter poem, the "something to look at" is the persona as Christ (19). While the theme of cyclical renewal is present in the book, the prologue merely points to it. What the prologue actually augurs for and emphasizes is the suffering and descent preceding the rise and resurrection ultimately experienced by the maturing persona herself. And the narrative invites the reader to share this suffering and descent through sharing the gaze of the author and persona in the recreation of a poignant moment of childhood pain.

As the adult Angelou relates this experience, she acknowledges that her young self, a victim of "well-known forgetfulness" (1), had not forgotten the lines; instead, she had more important things to remember, which should be a cue that the opening of *Caged Bird* is more than the re-creation pointed to above—that it will be a complexity created by a tension between narrator and subject, manifested by the tension between the vision of that adult and the gaze of the subject, the child.

Having been invited in to share the intensely personal gaze of young Maya, experiencing her pain with her as the shared gaze enables us to do, we participate in the text, in her embarrassment, in an entirely personal way. (...)

But our gaze is abruptly interrupted: the narrative hand suddenly holds us at a distance, permitting us to view her plight objectively, not personally: "If growing up is painful for the Southern Black girl, being aware of her displacement is the rust on the razor that threatens the throat. It is an unnecessary insult" (1). First person becomes third; pronouns are almost entirely omitted. The metaphor of the rusty razor wrests our attention from the eyes and feelings of young Maya. Angelou seems to consciously grip the problem of modernism here: the potential to lose ourselves in the mesmerizing gaze of the subject and so become subjects ourselves, inaccessible to the artistic vision competing with that compelling gaze. She commandingly pulls us back to observe from a distance, shifting her tense and forcing us to shift our viewing perspective, away from a familiar and thus comforting place in Angelou's and our own pasts into a discomforting, disconcerting present that makes indirect object of what had been subject, grammatically separating us from the southern black girl and so insuring that we can "see" her. Our, Maya's and our, personal recollection of that morning at the Colored Methodist Episcopal Church yields to the reality of victimization and its social consequences—and an appreciation of the art of the metaphor and the power of language, without which we remain subject and only subject. The gaze that reverts to the vision, through the alterations of language alone, makes problematic, and so keeps supple, the position of the audience in *Caged Bird*.

There is a remarkable similarity between the opening lines of *Caged Bird* and the opening page of *Their Eyes*: Angelou writes, "I hadn't so much forgot as I couldn't bring myself to remember. Other things were more important" (1). Hurston's narrator observes, you will recall, "Now, women forget all those things they don't want to remember, and remember everything they don't want to forget" (9). The privilege of memory drives both books; and their common intertextuality is present via their common visual techniques.

As the passages above exemplify, technically the visual works in both texts to lure us in and then push us back into our chairs. Such shifts in the reader's visual stance occur most directly, however, in *Caged Bird*: Angelou's language alternately lures us in, almost seductively, to share a gaze—connect ourselves personally—with the subject. And then we are forced out of the connection by language that diverts our attention to a vision of how difficult that connection is to maintain, and how dangerous to the ultimate success of the text.

Works by Maya Angelou

I Know Why the Caged Bird Sings, 1970.

Just Give Me a Cool Drink of Water 'fore I Diiie, 1971.

Gather Together in My Name, 1974.

Oh Pray My Wings Are Gonna Fit Me Well, 1975.

Singin' and Swingin' and Gettin' Merry Like Christmas, 1976.

And Still I Rise, 1978.

The Heart of a Woman, 1981.

Shaker, Why Don't You Sing?, 1983.

All God's Children Need Traveling Shoes, 1986.

Mrs. Flowers: A Moment of Friendship, 1986.

Poems: Maya Angelou, 1986.

Now Sheba Sings the Song, 1987.

I Shall Not Be Moved, 1990.

Wouldn't Take Nothing for My Journey Now, 1993.

Soul Looks Back in Wonder, 1993.

Life Doesn't Frighten Me, 1993.

On the Pulse of Morning, 1993.

The Complete Collected Poems of Maya Angelou, 1994.

My Painted House, My Friendly Chicken, and Me, 1994.

Soul Looks Back in Wonder, 1994.

Phenomenal Woman: Four Poems Celebrating Women, 1995.

A Brave and Startling Truth, 1995.

Kofi and His Magic, 1996.

Even the Stars Look Lonesome, 1997.

A Song Flung Up to Heaven, 2002.

Annotated Bibliography

Arensberg, Liliane K. "Death as Metaphor of Self in *I Know Why the Caged Bird Sings*," *CLA Journal* 20, no. 2 (December 1976): pp. 273–91.

While other critics have discussed Angelou's intense desire to fit in and not suffer the trials of being black, Arensberg goes further, calling Angelou's work a "personal confession of racial self-hatred." She points out the great significance of the beginning of the work.

Butterfield, Stephen. "Autobiographies of Black Women: Ida Wells, Maya Angelou, Anne Moody." In *Black Autobiography in America*. Amherst: University of Massachusetts Press, 1974: pp. 201–217.

Butterfield compares *I Know Why the Caged Bird Sings* to the work of other black women autobiographers—Ida Wells and Anne Moody—as well as to that of Richard Wright. While the others are more doggedly determined to describe the fight for their rights, Butterfield notes that part of Angelou stays untouched by white oppression and that she observes it from a distance. He marvels at her humor, compassion, and love of life.

Cudjoe, Selwyn R. "Maya Angelou: The Autobiographical Statement Updated." In *Reading Black, Reading Feminist: A Critical Anthology*. Ed. Henry Louis Gates, Jr. New York: Meridian, 1990: pp. 272–306.

Cudjoe writes about *I Know Why the Caged Bird Sings* as a logical outgrowth of political and social events of the Sixties, among them the growing feminist movement and the rift between black males and females. He sees Angelou's work and that of others of the time as concerned not just with examining black oppression but with an internal probing of the blacks' flawed personal development as well. Like other critics, Cudjoe also comments on Angelou's adult voice in the text, finding it damaging to the work.

Froula, Christine. "The Daughter's Seduction: Sexual Violence and Literary History," *Signs* 11, no. 4 (Summer 1986): pp. 621–44.

Froula explores what she sees as the limits imposed, from Homer through Freud, on male and female to silence women's speech when it threatens a father's power. Froula shows how *I Know Why the Caged Bird Sings* and *The Color Purple* refuse to abide by this convention.

Gilbert, Susan. "Maya Angelou's *I Know Why the Caged Bird Sings:* Paths to Escape," *Mount Olive Review* 1, no. 1 (Spring 1987): pp. 39–50.

Gilbert, author of many feminist works, sees Angelou's *I Know Why the Caged Bird Sings* and her other autobiographies as tales of great courage. Unlike other critics, Gilbert does not see Angelou's story as typical of the average black American woman's experience. She sees Angelou as breaking free of the provincialism that has ruined much of Southern and American literature. She sees Angelou's work as not overly egocentric and indicative of a rich, diverse life.

Hagen, Lyman B. *Heart of a Woman, Mind of a Writer, and Soul of a Poet: A Critical Analysis of the Writings of Maya Angelou.* Lanham, MD: University Press of America, Inc., 1996.

Hagen has written one of the few books written by one author covering Angelou's works. In it he places Angelou's works in an historical context and briefly reviews comments by numerous critics. He praises her storytelling technique and focuses on her use of humor through all five of her autobiographies.

Kent, George E. "Maya Angelou's *I Know Why the Caged Bird Sings* and Black Autobiographical Tradition," *Kansas Quarterly* 7, no. 3 (Summer 1975): pp. 71–78.

Kent, who has written on numerous black american authors, in this piece places *I Know Why the Caged Bird Sings* in the context of black autobiographical history. His vision differs from that of some of the other critics with this focus. He explains that black autobiography takes us on a journey through chaos, similar to the pattern established in slave narratives. He explains what makes *I Know Why the Caged Bird Sings* unique within this history—its recognition of the self's struggles and that the self must create its own order and coherence.

Kinnamon, Keneth. "Call and Response: Intertextuality in Two Autobiographical Works by Richard Wright and Maya Angelou." In *Studies in Black American Literature, Vol. II: Belief vs. Theory in Black American Literary Criticism*. Ed. William L. Andrews. Greenwood, FL: Penkevill Publishing Co., 1986: pp. 121–34.

Kinnamon expands on Robert B. Stepto's study of black American male writers in their search for freedom and education. Kinnamon compares Angelou's *I Know Why the Caged Bird Sings* to Richard Wright's *Black Boy* and looks at how their views may be different because of the authors' genders. He also explores the focus on community in both books.

Lionnet, Françoise. "Con Artists and Storytellers: Maya Angelou's Problematic Sense of Audience." In *Autobiographical Voices: Race, Gender, Self-Portraiture*. Ithica, N.Y.: Cornell University Press, 1989: pp. 130–166.

While other critics have commented on the fact that autobiography is not necessarily truth, Lionnet goes into detail here to explain that Angelou is torn even more than many other authors, struggling in her quest to write for both white and black audiences. Lionnet explores Angelou's technique in terms of the narrator's own love of literature, her use of religion, and her experience with various methods of communication deriving from folk traditions.

Lupton, Mary Jane. "Singing the Black Mother: Maya Angelou and Autobiographical Continuity," *Black American Literature Forum* 24, no. 2 (Summer 1990): pp. 257–276.

Lupton concentrates on motherhood and the relationship between mother and child as a unifier within *I Know Why the Caged Bird Sings*, within Angelou's other biographies, and connecting the five works to one another. She says the five volumes are also connected by the focus on creative work and motherhood.

O'Neale, Sondra. "Reconstruction of the Composite Self: New Images of Black Women in Maya Angelou's Continuing Autobiography." In *Black Women Writers (1950–1980)*, A Critical Evaluation. Ed. Mari Evans. Garden City, N.Y.: Doubleday, 1984: pp. 25–36.

O'Neale remarks that whereas there have been stereotyped visions of black women in literature, in *I Know Why the Caged Bird Sings* Angelou presents a new view, a composite she draws from the strong women in her book as well as from black history. Additionally, O'Neale examines how Angelou's self develops from knowledge gained through art and literature, and how Angelou realizes that to control her life she must rely on her own powerful intellect.

Saunders, James Robert. "Breaking Out of the Cage: The Autobiographical Writings of Maya Angelou," *The Hollins Critic* 28, no. 4 (October 1991): pp. 1–11.

Saunders reevaluates Stephen Butterfield's view of *I Know Why the Caged Bird Sings*, in what Saunders calls Butterfield's "seminal work," *Black Autobiography in America*. Saunders agrees that *Caged Bird* fits in with the slave narrative tradition, due especially to its focus on the importance of education, even for those in terrible circumstances. He disagrees with Butterfield, though, in terms of when confidence is truly attained in Angelou's work.

Smith, Sidonie Ann. "The Song of a Caged Bird: Maya Angelou's Quest After Self-Acceptance," *Southern Humanities Review* 7, no. 4 (Fall 1973): pp. 365–375.

Smith points out the persistence in black American autobiography on escaping enslavement. The place Angelou searches for is a "home" of acceptance, an escape from Stamps, Arkansas, where resistance is seen as impossible. She finds her own ways to resist and therefore becomes her own fully valued self.

Tangum, Marion M., and Marjorie Smelstor. "Hurston's and Angelou's Visual Art: The Distancing Vision and the Beckoning Gaze," *The Southern Literary Journal* 31, no. 1 (Fall 1998): pp. 80–97.

Tangum and Smelstor compare *I Know Why the Caged Bird Sings* and *Their Eyes Were Watching God*. In both, they say, the authors create a tension between their own authorial vision and that of the persona portrayed in the text. Through the authors' intensely personal description, readers are compelled to enter the experience of the persona but then are abruptly pulled out of the created world when the author provides comments on the described experiences, making us observers again rather than near participants.

Vermillion, Mary. "Reembodying the Self: Representations of Rape in *Incidents in the Life of a Slave Girl* and *I Know Why the Caged Bird Sings*," *Biography* 15, no. 3 (Summer 1992): pp. 243–260.

While other critics have commented on the way Angelou covers the rape in *I Know Why the Caged Bird Sings*, Vermillion examines it in terms of its historical context as well by comparing Angelou's book with the antebellum autobiography *Incidents in the Life of a Slave Girl*. Vermillion carefully observes how in both books the authors "reembody" the raped women. She pays careful attention to Angelou's foreshadowing and language.

Walker, Pierre A. "Racial Protest, Identity, Words, and Form in Maya Angelou's *I Know Why the Caged Bird Sings*," *College Literature* 22, no. 3 (October 1995): pp. 91–108.

Walker looks at *I Know Why the Caged Bird Sings* in the African-American literary tradition but focuses on Angelou's political message and accomplishment in the book. He points in detail to Angelou's strength in juxtaposing chapters, in having groups of chapters show a progression of theme, and in carefully orchestrating each chapter's design.

Contributors

Harold Bloom is Sterling Professor of the Humanities at Yale University and Henry W. and Albert A. Berg Professor of English at the New York University Graduate School. He is the author of over 20 books, including *Shelley's Mythmaking* (1959), *The Visionary Company* (1961), *Blake's Apocalypse* (1963), *Yeats* (1970), *A Map of Misreading* (1975), *Kabbalah and Criticism* (1975), *Agon: Toward a Theory of Revisionism* (1982), *The American Religion* (1992), *The Western Canon* (1994), and *Omens of Millennium: The Gnosis of Angels, Dreams, and Resurrection* (1996). *The Anxiety of Influence* (1973) sets forth Professor Bloom's provocative theory of the literary relationships between the great writers and their predecessors. His most recent books include *Shakespeare: The Invention of the Human* (1998), a 1998 National Book Award finalist, *How to Read and Why* (2000), *Genius: A Mosaic of One Hundred Exemplary Creative Minds* (2002), and *Hamlet: Poem Unlimited* (2003). In 1999, Professor Bloom received the prestigious American Academy of Arts and Letters Gold Medal for Criticism, and in 2002 he received the Catalonia International Prize.

Pamela Loos has researched or written more than twenty books of literary criticism, ranging from Goethe to Cormac McCarthy. She is the project editor of *Women Memoirists, Vol. II*, and also is the author of a young-adult biography of Maya Angelou.

Sidonie Ann Smith teaches English at the University of Michigan. She is the author of *Moving Lives: Twentieth-Century Women's Travel Writing*, as well as of other books. She has also edited or co-edited a number of titles covering women's autobiography and other literary topics.

Stephen Butterfield is the author of *Black Autobiography in America*.

George E. Kent, now deceased, was Professor of English at the University of Chicago. He was the author of *A Life of Gwendolyn Brooks* and *Blackness and the Adventure of Western Culture*.

Sondra O'Neale has taught African-American literature at Emory University. She is the author of *Jupiter Hammon and the Biblical Beginnings of African-American Literature*.

Joanie M. Braxton has taught American studies and English at the College of William and Mary. She is the joint author of a book on Maya Angelou and also has written *Black Women Writing Autobiography: A Tradition Within a Tradition*. Additionally, she is the co-editor of a title on the contemporary literary renaissance.

Françoise Lionnet teaches French at the University of California at Los Angeles. She has written *Autobiographical Voices: Race, Gender, Self-Portraiture* and other titles as well.

Dolly A. McPherson has taught at Wake Forest University. She has been the literary executor of the Maya Angelou Papers housed in the Z. Smith Reynolds Library at Wake Forest University. She has been a friend of Maya Angelou for more than forty years.

Mary Vermillion teaches humanities at Mount Mercy College in Cedar Rapids, Iowa.

Pierre A. Walker teaches English at Salem State College. He has written *Reading Henry James in French Cultural Contexts* and also is the editor of a work by Henry James.

Lyman B. Hagen is the author of *Heart of a Woman, Mind of a Writer, and Soul of a Poet* as well as of *Dee Brown*.

Marion M. Tangum has taught at Southwest Texas State University in San Marcos, Texas. She has done research on black American women writers, Faulkner and the South, and other later American literature.

Marjorie Smelstor is Provost/Director at the University of Missouri in Kansas City. She is the co-author of *Writing in the Social Studies*.

Acknowledgments

"The Song of a Caged Bird: Maya Angelou's Quest for Self-Acceptance" by Sidonie Ann Smith. From *Southern Humanities Review* 7, no. 4 (Fall 1973): pp. 369–370, 372–373. © 1973 by Auburn University. Reprinted by permission.

"Autobiographies of Black Women: Ida Wells, Maya Angelou, Anne Moody" by Stephen Butterfield. From *Black Autobiography in America*: pp. 203, 204, 205, 207–208. © 1974 by The University of Massachusetts Press. Reprinted by permission.

"Maya Angelou's *I Know Why the Caged Bird Sings* and Black Autobiographical Tradition" by George E. Kent. From *Kansas Quarterly* 7, no. 3 (Summer 1975): pp. 75–76, 77, 78. © 1975 by the *Kansas Quarterly*. Reprinted by permission.

"Reconstruction of the Composite Self: New Images of Black Women in Maya Angelou's Continuing Autobiography" by Sondra O'Neale. From *Black Women Writers (1950–1980)*, edited by Mari Evans: pp. 25–26, 31. © 1983 by Mari Evans. Reprinted by permission.

"A Song of Transcendence: Maya Angelou" by Joanne M. Braxton. From *Black Women Writing Autobiography*: pp. 181–182, 184–185, 192. © 1989 by Temple University. Reprinted by permission.

"Con Artists and Storytellers: Maya Angelou's Problematic Sense of Audience" by Françoise Lionnet. From *Autobiographical Voices: Race, Gender, Self-Portraiture*: pp. 130–132, 133. © 1989 by Cornell University. Reprinted by permission.

Index